D0848855

PIERS PLOWMAN STUDIES I

THE THEME OF GOVERNMENT IN PIERS PLOWMAN

The Theme of Government in Piers Plowman

ANNA P. BALDWIN

D. S. BREWER

© A. P. Baldwin 1981

First published 1981 by D. S. Brewer
240 Hills Road, Cambridge
an imprint of Boydell & Brewer Ltd.,
PO Box 9, Woodbridge, Suffolk IP12 3DF
and Wolfeboro, New Hampshire 03894-2069, USA

Reprinted 1987

British Library Cataloguing in Publication Data

Baldwin, Anna P.
   The theme of government in 'Piers Plowman'.
   (Langland studies, 1).
   2. Politics in literature
   I. Title   II. Series
   821'.1   PR2017.P6   80-49728

ISBN 0 85991 073 3

Printed and bound in Great Britain by
Short Run Press Ltd., Exeter

CONTENTS

ACKNOWLEDGEMENTS

My principal thanks must go to my Ph.D. supervisors at Cambridge. Dr R. Axton trained my interests and found me a subject. Professor W. Ullmann and Mr E. Miller disciplined my historical vagaries. Professor J. A. W. Bennett led me towards a new and more searching approach to the subject; without his great knowledge and kindness I could not have completed my work. My examiners, Dr A. C. Spearing and Professor G. Kane were helpful and informative. I was also extremely lucky in those whom I asked for advice. The legal aspect of this research could not have been begun without the extensive help of Dr D. E. C. Yale, Dr M. Pritchard, and Dr Baker of the Cambridge Law Faculty. I owe a particular debt to the kindness and assistance of Mr P. Dronke and Dr D. S. Brewer.

At York, where I rewrote my thesis (Cambridge 1976) into this book, the medievalists welcomed me into their stimulating community. Professor D. A. Pearsall and Professor R. B. Dobson have both given me detailed help and advice, and the late Professor E. Salter gave it a new direction. I shall miss her and Professor Bennett's inspiration and scholarship very much.

To these, and all my other teachers, this book is affectionately dedicated.

Anna P. Baldwin

INTRODUCTION

The aim of this book is to set Langland's discussions of government in their precise context in the fourteenth century, and to relate them to each other and to the poem as a whole. The context is historical, political and legal, and will often fill the gap left by the editors of the poem in explaining its many topical references.

In the Prologue and *Passus* II-IV[1] Langland describes England as a kingdom where social harmony and justice are threatened by Lady Meed and her powerful retinue. She represents a serious late medieval problem, and Langland indicates how it might be solved when the '*Visio* king' asserts his prerogative right to replace the corrupted Common Law by the Natural Law principles voiced by Reason and Conscience. (This was precisely the solution which Richard II's government also attempted — though with less success.) In the poem as a whole, however, only this ruler leads his community by asserting his authority. All the other governors who appear act more like subjects, and demonstrate to their fellow subjects the value of obedience to just laws. Thus Piers the Ploughman shows his fellow workers on the Half-acre how to work honestly and resist the 'waster', and he does not use the sanctions which fourteenth-century governments recommended for dishonest workmen. Nor does Christ use His royal prerogative to judge or pardon mankind until He has Himself obeyed the Old Testament Law, allegorized in the poem in terms of contemporary laws. Finally Conscience loses control of his fellow Christians in his kingdom of *Unitas* by failing to enforce the law of *redde quod debes*. These 'subject kings' return the responsibility for social or moral perfection from the ruler to the individual subject and Christian. This study will therefore centre on the problem of authority raised by Langland, that is: how can the absolutist ideal of monarchy embodied in the *Visio* king be made compatible with the more merciful, even democratic ideal practised by Piers, Conscience, and Christ?

Langland's ideals of government are the focus of his social criticism, and this is an aspect of the poem which has been rather neglected. It was in fact historians who first showed any real interest in what Langland had to say about his own society, but they tended to use the poem to illustrate their view of medieval history. Jusserand, finding many remarkable parallels between Langland's lines and Parliamentary records, decided that he had a profound respect for 'that grand phenomenon, the power of Parliament'.[2] Hilton used

Piers to demonstrate the relatively high status of fourteenth-century ploughmen, and Chadwick treated the poem as an anonymous series of vignettes of everyday life.[3]

If however history is put to the service of the poem, it becomes clear how very much an awareness of the historical and political context can elucidate Langland's lines. An understanding of Langland's many legal references is particularly useful; as Mathew wrote in 1948, 'it is characteristically medieval that all social problems should be expressed in terms of law'.[4] I will try to explain many individual obscurities, but only in the course of elucidating the whole sweep of Langland's allegories of government, which often reflect the form in which contemporary problems presented themselves in real life, or the way they might be resolved. Langland's solutions to the problems of society are essentially moral, and that has been fully demonstrated. But they are also political, and need to be understood in terms of contemporary political ideas, and Langland's own experience of law and government.

More recently literary critics have begun to investigate Langland's politics, most notably Donaldson, who asked whether the two versions of the 'Coronation Scene' in the B and C texts of the Prologue could possibly be written by the same author. His study is brilliant and illuminating, but it is only partial, and it does moreover concentrate, as Jusserand's did, on Langland's attitude to the Commons in government, which is more of a modern than a medieval preoccupation. In 1961 Bloomfield suggested that *Piers Plowman* was concerned more with the perfection of society (its 'apocalypse') than with the salvation of the individual, but he looked more closely at the role which temperance had to play in social development than at the role of government. In 1962 Lawlor drew attention to Langland's contrast between Christ, who embodies justice, and the *Visio* king, who had failed to establish justice in his kingdom. Recent studies by Kirk, Mathew, Kean, Birnes and Alford continue this interest in justice in *Piers Plowman*, and attempt to explain some of Langland's legal references.[5]

Valuable though these studies are they are only partial accounts of Langland's attitude to government. Yet whenever Langland describes a community of men he shows a leader trying to improve and help it, and these figures provide a structural link between the different sections of the poem. Through them Langland relates the social world, where the *Visio* king or Piers try to govern, with the whole created Universe, where Christ is king, and the world of the mind, where Conscience tries to rule. Just as the allegories of government need to be read as complete wholes if their topical relevance is to be fully understood, so also do they need to be related to each other if

Langland's own attitude to government is to be appreciated. For through these leaders he reveals not only political solutions to contemporary problems, but his hopes for man's ultimate perfectability.

I have based my study on the C-text, partly because it is probably Langland's final version, but largely because it has more to say about government, and says it more clearly, than the other two texts. I do however include analyses of relevant passages, notably from the B-text Prologue, which do not occur in C. I make the usual assumption of present scholars that the B-text was written in about 1378, and the C-text written some time after it before 1387 (when Thomas Usk, who quoted from it, was beheaded).[6] In other words, Langland was writing it during the political and social turmoils of Richard II's reign.

I

THE PROBLEM OF AUTHORITY

1. The ideal harmony

It has always been easier to say what good government should achieve than to explain how it should achieve it. English writers in prose and poetry in the later Middle Ages would probably have agreed that a society was, essentially:

> an elaborately articulated structure in which each member has his own appropriate rights and duties, assigned him not for his own sake, but for the sake of the well-being of the whole ... and directed to the common end by the supreme control of a single ruler.[1]

In an ideal community every member of every class or 'estate' fulfilled his duties and respected other's rights. Individually they obeyed God and their king, together they achieved unity and harmony.

When a preacher or moralist described how this ideal might be achieved, he often emphasised the moral duty of the individual to obey God and his governors. For example Gower describes the Golden age as a time when

> The citees knewen no debat
> The people stod in obeissance
> Under the reule of governance
> And pes which ryghtwisnesse keste,
> With charite tho stod in reste.[2]

A more secular approach might be to urge the king and his subjects to maintain harmony with one another, a harmony that was often characterised as 'lewte' (meaning loyalty) or 'truth' (in its sense of 'troth' or faithkeeping). A fifteenth-century translator of the popular *Secreta Secretorum* (an early medieval letter on the duties of kingship supposedly addressed by Aristotle to Alexander) uses both these words to translate *'fidem'*:

> Wytte thow, alexandyr, that by lewte and trowthe and feyth the Pepill byth vnyette, Citteis fulfillid, and mayntenyd lordshuppis. And yf feyth or lewte be forsake, than shall hit of the Pepill be and of lordshuppis As of wylde bestis, amonge woche euery olt hym abow hym to whom he is prere.[3]

A political writer in this tradition would then ask how the ruler can, through his personal obedience to God, or through his love for his people, lead the kingdom towards this ideal harmony.

Langland describes such a harmonious ideal at several places in *Piers Plowman*, but particularly in Reason's sermon (B.V.11-59, C.V.114-200), and when Grace equips the army of the Church (B.XI.215-261; C.XXI.215-261). In both places he emphasises the individual's moral responsibility to fulfil his role, and his social responsibility to keep faith (or 'treuthe') with his fellow subjects and king:

> 'And also,' quod Resoun, 'y rede ȝow ryche
> And comuners to acorde in alle kyn treuthe. . .
> Holde ȝow in vnite, and he þat oþer wolde
> Is cause of alle combraunces to confounde a reume.'
>
> C.V.182-3, 189-190

> 'Forthy,' quod Grace, 'or y go y wol gyue ȝow tresor . . .'
> And al he lered to be lele, and vch a craft loue oþere,
> Ne no boest ne debaet be among hem alle.
>
> C.XXI.225, 250-1

Of course Langland, like the preachers, poets and satirists who wrote 'estates satire' of this type,[4] only evokes the potential harmony of the estates to show how far his own society has departed from it. Like his contemporaries, Langland finds the source of England's ills in individuals' moral failures to fulfil their social duties. And in several important parts of *Piers Plowman* his approach becomes political, focusing on the individual who bore the greatest responsibility for fulfilling his own duties and for ensuring that his officers and people fulfilled theirs: the ruler.

In the fourteenth and fifteenth centuries many English writers, including Langland, produced examples of the 'mirror for princes' or *Fürstenspiegel* literature already popular on the continent.[5] Some of these works are indebted to the *Secreta Secretorum*, for example Wycliffe's *De Officio Regis* (1378), Book VII of Gower's *Confessio Amantis* (1386-1392), and Hoccleve's *Regement of Princes* (1411-12). Others however are influenced by the political passages in *Piers Plowman*, and so prove that these too have a place in this tradition. These include *Richard Redeless* (1399) and *Mum and the Sothsegger* (1406), the *Crowned King* (c.1415), and perhaps the poems of the *Digby Manuscript 102* (1400-1421?).[6] All these works advise the king morally, as a private person, and politically, as a wielder of power. Since his power would always be threatening to jeopardise his morality, they also discuss what restraints should be put upon it. Should the king, the elect of God, bear his heavy responsibility alone? Or should he share it with some more impersonal authority, such as the law, or even Parliament? In this chapter I will be considering how Langland theorises about the position and the role of the king, and will try to discover how much power he believes the king should have. His changing political opinions will be assessed by showing the use to which such theories were put, not only by other political writers but also by the actors in the stormy events of the fourteenth century.

Langland seems to give three possible answers to the question 'how much power should the king have?'. These may be described, somewhat freely, as a 'theocratic' theory, a theory of 'limited monarchy', and an 'absolutist' theory. (None of these are medieval terms.) The 'theocratic' theory is expressed by the king who appears at the end of *Passus* XXI (B.XIX) and makes rapacious demands which have to be restrained by Conscience. The theory of 'limited monarchy' is expressed in the 'Coronation Scene' in the Prologue of the B-text, but this satisfying balance of power seems to be cynically disproved by the Rat Fable which follows it. The 'absolutist' theory is all that we are left with in the C-text version of the 'Coronation Scene', but this seems depressingly conventional, and one hesitates to read it with any precision. Langland's answers to the problem of authority seem to be taken from three different political traditions. In which does he finally believe?

2. The tyrant king: C.XXI.465-479 (B.XIX.465-479)

It seems perverse to open the discussion by analysing one of the last descriptions of government in the poem. But it will be easier to establish what Langland's political ideals are, when we have rejected what they are not. For the king who describes his style of government in C.XXI.465-476 (which is virtually identical to B.XIX.465-473) is a bad king — almost a tyrant. The appearance in the world of rulers like him is but one indication of the corruption of the society of the early Church which Grace and Piers have founded on the four Cardinal Virtues.

It was a society, it will be remembered, in which every craft was to 'loue opere' (XXI.250). Yet as soon as Grace and Piers have gone to

7

'tulye treuthe' (334) in other societies of the world, the crafts become crafty and learn how to exploit each other. In the process they corrupt the Cardinal Virtues themselves. A greedy lord uses his *spiritus intellectus* (or as Piers sowed it, his *spiritus prudencie*) to revise his reeve's accounts in his own favour, and uses his *spiritus fortitudinis*, as brute force, to make him pay the difference (459-464). Instruction as to how this should be done had been given in several respectable books on estate management.[7] Following his example, a greedy king conveniently forgets that *spiritus iusticie* subjected even kings to the law (303-9), and claims that in fact it entitles him to take whatever he wants from his subjects:

> And thenne cam þer a kyng and bi his corone saide:
> 'Y am kyng with croune the comune to reule
> And holy kyrke and clerge fro cursed men to defende.
> And yf me lakketh to lyue by, þe lawe wol þat y take hit
> Ther y may hastilokest hit haue, for y am heed of lawe
> And ʒe ben bote membres and y aboue alle.
> And sethe y am ʒoure alere heued y am ʒoure alere hele
> And holy churche cheef helpe and cheuenteyn of þe comune
> And what y take of ʒow two y take hit at þe techynge
> Of *Spiritus iusticie*, for y iuge ʒow alle
> So y may boldely be hoseled for y borwe neuere
> Ne craue of my comune bote as my kynde asketh.'
>
> C. XXI. 465-476

This king is making the assumptions of a 'theocratic' monarch, the representative of God on earth which the Roman Emperor had claimed to be. The 'Civilians' had acquainted the medieval world with the political concepts of Justinian's *Corpus Juris Civilis*, although they were largely irrelevant to actual political conditions. Langland's king is using some of them when he claims to be not only head of law and head of the body politic, but different in 'kynde' from the rest of the community. Unlike the humble mortals he judges, all his actions embody *Spiritus iusticie*; in other words, he is 'animate justice' and infallible. Like the Emperor, the law may lie in his will, and so, like the Emperor, he may ignore the ordinary laws of property and take what he likes from his people.[8]

Now in England such imperialist claims to be above the laws, particularly the laws of property, were associated with tyranny. Richard II in particular was accused of taking his subjects' property illegally, and the Parliament which assented to his deposition defended its actions partly by quoting the theocratic way in which he had supposedly spoken:

> he had often said and affirmed that the life of every one of his lieges, together with the lands, tenements, goods and chattels of such men, was subject to his own pleasure, apart from any [lawful] forfeiture.[9]

8

As this Parliament pointed out, an English king should not rule according to his will but according to the laws which he swore at his coronation to defend. The imperialist claims of the king in *Passus* XXI are therefore tyrannical in an English context.

On the other hand Conscience, the true king of *Unitas*, does not think it would take much to turn this tyrant into an acceptable sovereign. In view of the weight which Langland gives to Conscience's opinions throughout the poem, it will be worth seeing in more detail how Conscience legalises royal authority. He tells the king that he may supply himself from the public purse so long as he obeys two conditions. He must use the money to defend and rule the kingdom, and he must let reason and truth direct his rulership:

> 'In condicioun,' quod Conscience, 'þat þou þe comune defende
> And rewle thy rewme in resoun riht wel and in treuthe,
> Than haue thow al thyn askyng as thy lawe asketh.
> *Omnia sunt tua ad defendendum sed non ad deprehendendum.*
> C.XXI.477-9

The first of these conditions (that the king should defend the kingdom) distinguishes between the king's personal needs and those of the state. A theocratic monarch need not make such a distinction, and in the next *Passus* Need, who represents Necessity itself, claims that the king had been right to take what he personally needed from his people (C.XXII.6-9) because:

> nede ne hath no lawe ne neuere shal falle in dette.
> C.XXII.10

The king had indeed claimed that he never borrowed (XXI.475) and so, presumably, never fell in debt, because he was entitled to supply all his needs.

Now the principle of necessity could be used to override the normal laws of property in cases of personal emergency. As the Canon Law said, 'necessity makes the unlawful licit', and Aquinas explained that this was due to a Natural Law right to survival:

> What pertains to human law can in no way detract from what pertains to Natural or Divine law ... If ... there is such urgent and evident necessity ... of necessary sustenance ... then [a man] may take what is necessary from another person's goods, either openly or by stealth. Nor is this, strictly speaking, fraud or robbery.[10]

However, Langland's king is scarcely in any personal danger of starvation, and so cannot justify his actions in terms of what Need will call the 'lawe of kynde' (XXII.18).

Although Conscience does not condone the king disregarding the laws of property for his personal convenience, he does hint that the

9

country's defence could justify such actions. It was in fact generally accepted that in cases of national emergency, such as war, a king could invoke the principle of necessity to override the normal laws, and for example tax the unwilling clergy. Both Ockham and Wycliffe advised their kings in these terms, and recently, during an invasion scare in 1371, two friars had come before Parliament to say that 'all possessions, including those of the clergy as of others, should be in common in all cases of necessity'.[11] The king in C.XXI had also intended to tax both clergy and laity. Conscience accordingly insists that he should ask for such funds in order to help the nation defend itself from its enemies (*'ad defendendum'*) and not in order to bleed the nation dry (*'ad deprehendendum'*) for his personal gratification. And Langland in this rejects the theocratic principle that the king's private and public persons are indistinguishable. The law cannot bow to his personal desires, or even his personal needs.

Conscience is rejecting the same theocratic principle when he makes his other condition: that the king should be ruled by reason and truth (478). A theocratic monarch claimed to speak on God's behalf, but any other kind of sovereign, however powerful, would have to agree to be bound at least by divine laws, if he were not to become a tyrant. This was the view of the Civilians who adapted Classical political theories to apply to the real German Emperor. They taught that although he was head of the laws which he gave to his subjects, he could only dispense with them himself when justified by Reason. The Emperor Frederick II himself admitted that:

> although our imperial majesty is free from all laws, it is nevertheless not altogether above the judgment of Reason, herself the mother of all laws.[12]

A sovereign who is restrained only by Reason or Divine Law may be called an 'absolute' monarch, that is to say, a monarch whom only God, and not any political institution, can compel to act in conformity with justice and law. He would not have the infallibility of the theocratic monarch, but would rather be a 'dual person', whose morality as an individual would necessarily influence his public acts as king.

If the king in *Passus* XXI does obey Conscience, then his position will be that of an absolute monarch. One can judge this by comparing these lines with a passage from Wycliffe's *De Officio Regis* (1378), one of the few English treatises to develop an absolutist theory of sovereignty. Like Langland's Conscience, Wycliffe allows the king

> in times of his realm's or his own necessity [to] take the temporal possessions both of the laity and of the clergy. For thus does the heart in its necessity draw heat and moisture from every possible member.[13]

10

However, although the king should have ultimate authority over the law of the land, he too should be subject to reason and truth:

> Then [the king] should note how law, like the reason or truth which is above all human power, binds all men, and even binds the humanity of Christ, although according to His Divinity He is above all law . . .14

Langland's king, like Wycliffe's, has a double nature. Although he is publicly the head of law, he is also only a man, and in no sense the embodiment of *Spiritus iusticie*, which should rather rule his actions and persuade him to obey the law. Through invoking reason and truth, Conscience has restored *Spiritus iusticie* to the position of supremacy which Piers originally gave it:

> *Spiritus iusticie* spareth nat to spille hem þat ben gulty
> And for to corecte the kyng, and the kyng falle in any agulte.
>   C.XXI.303-4

Although England was familiar with the theory of absolute monarchy through the writings of theologians such as Wycliffe, her own constitution was somewhat different. It had its roots in feudal land law, and was first analysed by lawyers rather than theologians. Feudal law rested on the assumption that there was a contract between the lord and his vassal, which was dissolved if either party flagrantly ignored his customary obligations. The king was landlord as well as ruler of England, and as such was obliged to ask for the counsel of his tenants-in-chief (the 'magnates') if he wished to rely on their aid and support. There thus developed comparatively early in England the principle that the king was 'limited' by past customs and, to a certain extent, by the decisions of his Great Council of magnates. The customs developed into a complex body of Common Law, and the Great Council developed into Parliament. And on more than one occasion in the fourteenth century this Parliament forced the king to obey the laws which he made, not by himself, but with his magnates and commons. By the fifteenth century, Fortescue was proudly distinguishing this English type of government, which he called *dominium politicum et regale*, from the *dominium regale* (absolute monarchy, as we would call it) practised in France.15

If the king in *Passus* XXI is allowed by Conscience to retain an absolutist, if not a theocratic position, the king who is crowned in the Prologue to the B-text seems to hold the more limited powers of the actual English monarch. He is bound by the law which he makes with his 'commune'. I will now discuss this passage (B.Prol.112-145), for it was so thoroughly revised for the C-text that it may be considered as another of Langland's rejected answers to the problem of

11

authority. But it will be far more difficult to see why he rejected this theory of 'limited monarchy' than it was to see why he rejected the theocratic theory expressed by the tyrant king in *Passus* XXI.

3. The aspiring commune: B.Prol.112-145

The first *Passus* of *Piers Plowman* demonstrates, among other things, the need for a just authority in the State. In a passage of loose estates-satire (B.Prol.20-111; C.Prol.22-94) Langland divides the occupations of the folk of the field into the valuable (such as those of the ploughman and genuine hermit) and the useless or even harmful (such as those of the 'Iaperes and Iangeleres', or of most of the beggars and clerics). This opening exposition of society reveals not only the religious vacuum created by a corrupt Church, but also the social injustice caused by indulgence towards these 'wastours' (B.22, C.24). Accordingly, after he has castigated the bishops and leaders of the Church for their failure to purify the religious life of the community (B.Prol.87-111, C.Prol.85-138), Langland introduces those who are responsible for enforcing social justice through law.

In Landland's first text of the 'Coronation Scene' where the king is introduced and advised how to rule (B.Prol.112-145), it is not only the king who is given the authority to organise and control the secular community. The 'commune' also seem to have some power. Donaldson has worked out from the rest of the poem that this word generally means 'community', and he directs our attention to its political role.[16] In the first place it actually gives the king his authority:

> Thanne kam þer a kyng; kny3thod hym ladde;
> Might of þe communes made hym to regne.

B.Prol.112-3

Even more strikingly, the community helps the king to make the law:

> The kyng and þe commune and kynde wit þe þridde
> Shopen lawe and leaute, ech [lif] to knowe his owene.

B.Prol.121-2

In these lines the king, like the English monarch, seems to be sharing his powers with Parliament. Then, having let a lunatic and an angel mouth a few platitudes, a Goliard confirms this impression of 'limited' monarchy by stressing that the king is below, not above, the law of the land;

> 'Dum rex a regere dicatur nomen habere
> Nomen habet sine re nisi studet iura tenere.'[17]

B.Prol.141-2

12

The only discordant note is struck by the commons themselves, for they seem prepared to accept the most wilful decrees of their monarch as law:

'Precepta Regis sunt nobis vincula legis'. [18]

B.Prol.145

The four passages quoted in this paragraph thus, with only one exception, establish a model of limited monarchy: a king who shares with the community the power to make the law and the inconvenience of being bound by it.

Now these are the four passages which are either revised or cut from the C-text, where the king reigns by the might of the knights, not the commons (C.Prol.140), does not share his law-making power with the community, and hears only the 'platitudes' spoken in the B-text by the lunatic and the angel (C.Prol.147-157). These changes have been illuminatingly discussed by Donaldson, but as he is endeavouring to prove that the two texts were written by a single poet, he plays down the differences between them. He argues that since analogues to the statements in both texts (with the exception of the Goliard's speech) can be found in the coronation *Ordos* or Rituals[19] of the previous four hundred years, they must all be equally safe, indeed 'middle of the road' in their politics. But although I do not of course question Donaldson's conclusion that one author wrote both texts, I would argue that they do embody different political traditions, and that this can be demonstrated by using a wider and more contemporary context than the coronation *Ordos* on their own can provide.

Leaving aside for the moment the passages in the B-text which also occur in C, it will be remembered that three passages in the B-text 'limited' the monarch's power (112-3, 121-2, 139-142). All three statements can be closely paralleled in Bracton's essay on kingship in *De Legibus et Consuetudinibus Angliae*, the first and easily the most influential attempt to describe the English constitution as it really was, and one that was still widely used and transcribed in the fourteenth century.[20] It may even have been from this true scholar of coronation *Ordos* that Langland got the verbal echoes noted by Donaldson. Since *De Legibus* is, as far as an early thirteenth-century work can be, a description of a *limited* monarchy, this analogue confirms our impression that this is the sort of State described in the Prologue to the B, though not to the C text.

Bracton begins the section on kingship with a traditional ecclesiastical statement of the king's responsibility to do both justice and mercy (corresponding to the speeches of the lunatic and the angel in the B-text). He immediately warns the king however that true justice,

13

by which every man is 'restored to that which is his own', is the product not of the king's will but of law, and law is made only 'with the counsel of his magnates, deliberation and consultation having been had thereon, the king giving it authority'. Bracton in fact gives precisely the same role to the 'counsel of . . . magnates' (in Parliament) as Langland gives to 'the commune' (presumably the whole community – including the magnates – represented in Parliament) and 'kynde wit':

> The kyng and þe commune and kynde wit þe þridde
> Shopen lawe and leaute, ech [lif] to knowe his owene.
>
> C.Prol.121-2

In this instance Bracton only reinforces the impression of limited monarchy which was given by the analogue which Donaldson provided for this couplet: the king's oath to 'uphold and guard the rightful laws and customs which the community of your realm will choose'. For this clause was hardly the conservative truism which Donaldson implies it was. It was one of the three clauses sworn to for the first time by Edward II, and the Lords of Parliament who later assented to his deposition, claimed that his failure to hold to his oath and rule according to law disqualified his right to the throne – a claim repeated in the Articles 'deposing' Richard II in 1399.[21] A community which really does help to 'shopen lawe and leaute' can also dethrone its king.

Bracton goes on to give another version of the very etymology of 'king' which the Goliard uses in the B-text Prologue. In Bracton's text the limitations on the monarch's power which the etymology implies are more explicit than in Langland's:

> For he is called *rex* not from reigning but from ruling well. . . Let him, therefore, temper his power by law . . . for the law of mankind has decreed that his own laws bind the lawgiver . . . and he ought properly to yield to the law what the law has bestowed upon him, for the law makes him king.[22]

The radical implications of this argument may also be gathered from its use in political poetry attacking misgovernment. It appears for example in the *Song of Lewes*, which accused Henry III of not ruling according to law and his parliament:

> *Dicitur uulgariter: ut rex uult, lex uadit*
> *Veritas uult aliter, nam lex stat, rex cadit.*[23]

A much closer version of the couplet Langland used occurs in a poem of 1388 which blames Richard II and his counsellors for the lawlessness of society as a whole:

O rex, si rex es, rege te, vel eris sine re rex
Nomen habes sine re, nisi te recteque regas rex.[24]

The explosive element in these couplets in their implication that the king only has authority under the law, which, when the community is also given a share in making the law, effectively limits the king's power.

I am not suggesting that Langland had read Bracton, though that is very possible. All the analogue demonstrates is the political tenor of Langland's 'Coronation Scene' in the B-text. Even if he had never heard of Bracton, he has used precisely those arguments which associate the lawyer with the theory of limited monarchy, and which fourteenth-century politicians and poets used for the same purpose. In omitting these passages from the C-text, he is turning his back on that model of government.

4. The triumph of absolutism in the C-text Prologue: C. Prol. 139-216

In the C-text of the 'Coronation Scene', the 'commune' is given no political power: it neither makes the king reign (C.Prol.140), nor helps make the law. Instead it is occupied merely with supplying the kingdom with necessities (C.Prol.142-6). Neither are human laws given authority over the king; they are not even mentioned. The advice the king is left with puts no political restraints upon him, but only moral and religious ones. Indeed it encourages him to take full responsibility for the social justice of his kingdom, *whether or not* he acts through law.

First of all 'Kynde Witt' (a less equivocal presence than the 'lunatik' who has the lines in the B-text) prays that the king will:

> 'lede so þy londe þat Lewte þe louye
> And for thy rightful ruylynge be rewardid in heuene.'
>
> C.Prol.149-150

'Lewte' is derived from the Latin *legalitas* through the Old French *lealte*, and has a range of meanings from 'justice' or 'legality' to 'loyalty' and 'faithkeeping'.[25] Even if we interpret it here as a personification of legality, the king's leadership and rightful ruling are the cause and not the effect of his conformity to law. If he rules justly, legality itself will love him. Conscience, who follows Kynde Witt even urges the king to override the law by the use of his prerogative of mercy:

15

'Sum Rex, sum princeps: neutrum fortasse deinceps.
O qui iura regis christi specialia regis,
Hoc vt agas melius, iustus es, esto pius.'[26]

C.Prol.152-4

To be sure, the sentiments expressed by Kynde Witt and Conscience are commonplace. The Latin lines can be found in the manuscript of an early fourteenth-century sermon; Bracton, quoting a twelfth-century Coronation Oath, says much the same thing.[27] Langland is only restating the double duty of kings to do both justice and mercy. Aquinas puts this succinctly in his very influential *De Regimine Principium* (mid-thirteenth century):

> A king, then, should realise that he has assumed the duty of being to his kingdom what the soul is to the body and what God is to the universe. If he thinks attentively upon this point he will, on the one hand, be fired with zeal for justice, seeing himself appointed to administer justice throughout his realm in the name of God, and, on the other hand, he will grow in mildness and clemency, looking upon the persons subject to his government, as the members of his own body.[28]

It is however clear from Aquinas' remarks that such a responsibility is best fulfilled by an absolute king, who is to his kingdom 'what God is to the universe'. Only absolute power allows a king to choose between justice and mercy. Aquinas modifies this political position at other points in his works, but Langland has left the speeches of Kynde Witt and Conscience to stand on their own in the C-text. However conventional their words, these figures are in fact suggesting, like the absolutist canonist Baldus, that 'a good king is better than a good law'.[29]

The absolutist impression is strengthened by the fact that it is only Kynde Witt and Conscience who say this. They are not independent advisors as the 'commune', the angel, or even the lunatic were; they exist rather within the king's own soul. Indeed several critics have shown that they correspond fairly closely to the *ratio* (also represented by the character 'Reason') and the *conscientia* which (with *synderesis*, the intuitive habit of doing good) make up the moral faculty in Aquinas' well-known analysis of the soul.[30] If the king is to be guided by his *ratio* and *conscientia*, then Langland's political position in the C-text of the 'Coronation Scene' differs little from that at the end of C. XXI, where the tyrant-king was restrained by Conscience alone. At best, both are God-fearing but absolute monarchs, taking full responsibility for the harmony and justice of their kingdoms.

That Langland had a preference for absolutism is confirmed by his odd interpretation of the rat fable (C. Prol. 165-216; B. Prol. 146-217).

When Nicholas Bozon or Bishop Brinton used the fable, as Langland would probably have known, the rats' failure to bell their cat represented 'the pusillaminity of subjects'.[31] But in Langland's version the rats and mice seem to represent not the whole community of subjects, but only one rather destructive element in it, like the rats and mice in a real household. Similarly, the cat may appear as a tyrant to the narrow rodent community, but in the wider community of the household his control is very necessary:

> 'For many mannys malt we muys wolde distruye
> And þe route of ratones of reste men awake
> Ne were þe cat of þe court and ȝonge kitones toward'.
>
> C. Prol. 213-5

Because the fable is poised in this way between allegory and description of real life, it is impossible to feel much sympathy for the pretensions of creatures who are still clearly vermin. The rats' attempt to bell the cat may seem at first sight to represent Parliament's attempt to control a cruel tyrant 'for . . . comune profyt' (167, 184). But the rats are only a rapacious part of the wider community; all they really want is to be 'lordes a-lofte' themselves (175). This may well indicate Langland's opinion of Parliament, which certainly does not seem here to champion the best interests of the whole community. As one mouse points out with Langland's overt approval, the loss of an effective cat would harm the 'comune profit' (201) of men, mice, and even the rats themselves:

> 'For hadde ȝe ratones ȝoure reik, ȝe couthe nat reule ȝow-suluen.'
>
> C. Prol. 216

Even a just king will seem a tyrant to those who incur his justice.

In the B-text the 'court' (149) where the cat lives seems to mean the king's palace. The C-text version of the fable however is set in a corrupt law-court (C. Prol. 158-164) so that it seems to demonstrate the danger of depriving the judge, as well as the king, of the 'teeth and claws' he needs to execute his authority. The rats' plan to offer their cat a silver collar and bell (which, as the mice in Bozon's fable had ingratiatingly said, would only do him honour) seems dangerously reminiscent of the great lords' gifts of collars and liveries to the knights — or the officials and judges — who joined their retinues:[32]

> 'Y haue seyen grete syres in cytees and in townes
> Bere beyus of bryghte gold al aboute here nekkes
> And colers of crafty werk, bothe knyghtes and squieres.'
>
> C. Prol. 177-9

If belling the cat is tantamount to bribing the executive or the judicature with fees and liveries, then the wiser mouse is obviously right to prefer his cat unbelled. However tyrannical the authority which executes the laws, it is better than one which has so lost its indepen-dence as to be no authority at all.

In both texts then the rat fable shows the inevitability and the desirability of absolutism. But whereas in the B-text the fable under-cuts the 'Coronation Scene''s gestures towards limited monarchy, in the C-text the appearance of an absolute monarch is followed quite consistently by an absolutist fable. It is true that medieval writers on kingship, whatever their political colours, were apt to mouth con-ventionally absolutist sentiments before they got down to their real opinions. The C-text revision of the Prologue, however, seems too precise and too comprehensive to be merely a conventional intro-duction. It must therefore be concluded that this important statement of Langland's political theory is purposely closer to the absolutist ideas developed by the civil lawyers, or by theologians like Wycliffe, than to the traditions and practices of his own country.

5. The triumph of absolutism in the poem as a whole

Before I test this surprising conclusion against the actual behaviour of the *Visio* king when he attempts to reform his kingdom, it would be as well to glance at other passages in which Langland discusses whether the king should share his power either with the community, or with the law. The most significant comments on the role of the community are made in the C-text addition to Conscience's long harangue in *Passus* III — perhaps written after Langland had revised the Prologue and clarified his views. It contains this statement of the ideal which good government should aim to achieve:

> 'Ac relacoun rect is a ryhtful custume,
> As a kyng to clayme the comune at his wille
> To folowe and to fynde hym and fecche at hem his consayl
> That here loue to his lawe thorw al þe londe acorde.
> So comune claymeth of a kyng thre kyne thynges,
> Lawe, loue and lewete, and hym lord antecedent,
> Bothe heued and here kyng, haldyng with no parteyȝe
> Bote standynge as a stake þat stikede in a mere
> Bytwene two [londes] for a trewe marke.'[33]

C.III.373-381

Like the usual idealisations of society to which I referred at the beginning of this chapter, this ideal of 'Lawe, loue and lewete' gives equal weight to justice ('lawe', and 'lewete' in the sense of legality) and allegiance ('loue', and 'lewete' in the sense of loyalty). It is

18

significant however that the king is to *give* this social ideal to his people, and moreover must remain 'lord antecedent' in order to ensure impartial justice. The 'comune's' part in this 'relacoun rect' is simply to provide obedience and provisions – which is roughly what the tyrant-king in *Passus* XXI expected of them.

The absolutism of this political ideal is highlighted by comparing it with some lines from *Richard Redeless*, a poem which reuses Langland's idiom for different political ends. The author does not expect the king to *give* 'lawe, loue and lewete' to his people, he should rather *accept*, as a condition for rulership, the 'lewte and loue' which his peers once offered him (I.44) and will restore only if he keeps the laws of the land:

> Of alegeaunce now lerneth / a lesson oþer tweyne
> Wher-by it standith / or stablithe moste –
> By dride, or be dyntis / or domes vntrewe, . . .
> By pillynge of ȝoure peple / ȝoure prynces to plese, . . .
> Or be ledinge of lawe / with loue well ytemprid.[34]

By contrast, Conscience in *Piers Plowman* seems to believe that both law and social harmony are principally the responsibility of the king.

If Langland does not seem to trust the community to share the king's power as much as some of his contemporaries did, neither does he trust the law to limit the king's power. Indeed when Conscience returns to the subject of government at the end of *Passus* III in his famous 'political prophecy'[35] (C.III.436-481; B.III.284-330), he suggests that any law not under the protection of a just ruler inevitably becomes corrupted by Meed (here meaning 'bribery'):

> 'Muche euel is thorw Mede mony tymes ysoffred
> And letteth the lawe thorw here large ȝeftes.
> Ac kynde loue shal come ȝut and Conscience togyderes
> And maky of lawe a laborer, suche loue shal aryse
> And such pees among þe peple and a parfit treuthe . . .'
>
> C.III.449-453

The law which needs to be made a labourer is clearly not the impartial law imposed by a king in 'relacoun rect' with his subjects, but medieval legal practice in all its imperfection. The true king, according to Conscience, so far from being limited by the Common Law of England, would actually abolish the jury which had become indispensable to its working:

> 'Shal nother kyng ne knyght, constable ne mayre
> Ouerkarke þe comune ne to þe court sompne
> Ne potte men in panele to do men plihte here treuthe,
> But aftur þe dede þat is ydo the doom shal recorde
>
> C.III.467-470

In Conscience's ideal kingdom it is the king and his 'iustice . . . Trewe-tonge' (473-4), using the autocratic process of 'judgment by record',[36] and not the normal processes of Common Law, who guarantees justice.

It is incidently worth noting that this passage is modelled on prophecies of the Millennium (Isaiah 2:2-5) and the Second Coming of King David (Jeremiah 30:8-10; Amos 9:11-15, interpreted by Christian commentators as the Second Coming of Christ). It does not however use apocalyptic images to celebrate Langland's own king, as many other 'political prophecies' did, but to provide a Divine contrast to the worldly events in the *Visio* king's court.[37] At the heart of the most political part of *Piers Plowman* Langland points away from human society towards Christ, the type of the ideal king.

In a similar prophecy in the next *Passus*, Reason still further reduces the status of law:

> 'And yf ȝe worche it in werke y wedde bothe myn handes
> That lawe shal ben a laborer and lede afelde donge
> And loue shal lede thi land as the leef lyketh.'

C.IV.143-5

As Miss Kean has pointed out, leaute (which she translates as justice) and love are given pre-eminence over law in such passages. In this context it may be observed that Trajan, the ideal pagan ruler, also seems to put leaute and love above law:

> 'For lawe withouten leutee, ley þer a bene!
> Or eny science vnder soone, the seuene ars and alle,
> Bote loue and leute hem lede . . .'

C.XII.91-3

Langland does indeed demonstrate in *Passus* II-IV, as I will show in my next chapter, that by itself law is immensely susceptible to Meed. Unless the king protects it, it cannot achieve that 'loue and lewete' characteristic of a good community. Langland was too aware of the difference between the idea of law, and actual legal practice to be able to echo his contemporaries' desire to give law an independent authority over the king. In the same way, he was perhaps too aware of the short-comings of the individual members of the community to trust them with any share in the power that God has committed to kings. For him, a king who rules with Parliament according to the law is less likely to achieve the ideal social harmony, than a king who rules independently according to his own idea of justice. That is all very well, but how is he to decide what justice is? and can he be prevented from disregarding justice and becoming a tyrant?

Langland consistently gives the same answers to these questions. The king learns justice from the faculties within his own soul, and he cannot be forced to obey their dictates. It was neither the community nor the law which restrained the tyrant-king in *Passus* XXI, but Conscience, who told him to rule 'in resoun . . . and in treuthe' (478). It was not the 'comune', but 'Kynde Witt' (used probably as another name for Reason) and Conscience who advised the king in the C-text 'Coronation Scene'. And it will be Reason and Conscience who continue to advise him during the turmoils which overtake his kingdom in *Passus* II-IV. Their advice does not contradict the law, but rather indicates the true justice which the law has failed to impose.

Reason and Conscience, as I have said, were two of Aquinas' three faculties of the soul. A man desires to do good (by the intuitive habit of *synderesis*); he thinks what would be good (by *ratio*); and only then does he decide to act (by *conscientia*). Several critics have demonstrated that Langland's Reason, like Aquinas' *ratio*, has more authority than Conscience. Reason thinks and understands; Conscience attempts to put his wisdom into practice, and can be rather lost on his own.[38] The king, like any other moral individual, relies on them both, but particularly on Reason. Does Langland then believe that the problems of authority are solved simply by the private morality of the ruler? Such a conclusion is inevitable if we interpret Reason and Conscience only psychologically. But the king is also a public person, and in his case Reason in particular has a political role which has not been properly understood, although here too Aquinas shows the way.

Although in *De Regimine Principium* Aquinas inclined to an absolutist view of monarchy, in the *Summa Theologica* he developed and expanded the concept of the Divine Law which should limit the actions of even the most absolute king. He showed that only part of this Divine Law was expressed through revelation and taught by the Church. The other part, which was what he understood as the 'Natural Law', was available to all men through their *ratio naturalis*. As the Classical writers had said, even the animals obey the Natural Law in regulating their social and family lives. But unlike animals, men 'have a certain share in the divine reason itself. This participation in the eternal law by rational creatures is called the natural law.'[39] Aquinas and his followers developed this compendious idea into a whole system of natural duties and rights, such as the duty to honour contracts, and the right to life and property. A king who, like the tyrant-king in *Passus* XXI, failed to observe his subjects' property rights could not expect their obedience. More generally, unless the laws he made were just, that is, in accordance with the principles of Natural Law, they would not be lawful at all.

In England the concept of Natural Law was usually referred to as 'Reason'. As early as 1522 St German pointed out that 'when any-thyng is groundyd vpon the lawe of nature: [the English] say that reason wyll that such a thyng be don.' The truth of St German's insight is shown in the *Year Books* of the English Central Courts, which explained for example in 1341, that Reason is the basis of all law. Or again, when the townsmen of Rye adopted a reference to *'jura naturalia'* from the Winchelsea Custumal into their own Borough Laws in the fifteenth century, they called them 'the laws of natural reason'.[40]

Langland himself seems to have been aware of Reason's association with Natural Law theory, because Will is shown in C.XIII.142-154 (B.XI.335-344) how animals' family lives are ruled by Reason, which cannot carry a purely moral sense here because animals have no souls. Langland may even have read in the *Summa Theologica* itself that it is a man's *ratio naturalis* which teaches him the Natural Law, for does he not give Kynde Witt a key role in founding the kingdom in the Prologue (141, 142, 144, 147)? It is probable that he saw Reason as the most important counsellor a king could have, because without Reason the state itself lacks legality.

Yet we are brought back to the difference between the political counsellors in *Piers Plowman* and in poems influenced by it, such as *Richard Redeless* or *Mum and the Sothsegger*. In these later poems it is Parliament, or at least wise councillors ('Witt', the 'Sothsegger') who speak with the voice of Reason, and they generally tell the king to obey the laws of the land.[41] But as I have already indicated, and will develop in the next two chapters, Langland mistrusts both the corruptible processes of law, and the corrupted members of his Parliament. In the Vision of Lady Meed, only the king attempts to eradicate injustice and re-establish his kingdom on the basis of Reason. And this replacement of law as the instrument of justice, by the king's direct imposition of the Natural Law principles of justice, represents a specific judicial development in the later fourteenth century, and one which gives another dimension to the characters of Reason and Conscience.

In the later Middle Ages the English king began to exercise his ancient prerogative to do justice and mercy irrespective of law, by a new use of his own highest councils: Parliament, the Privy Council, and the Court of Chancery. These councils began to sit as courts which were not bound by Common Law procedures, but brought the principles of justice to bear upon individual cases in individual (though quickly regulated) ways. Eventually this development was to be known as 'equity', but in the fourteenth century it was often described as judgment according to 'right and reason' (*'droit & reson'*) – that is to say, according to the Natural Law which the Common Law had failed to enact. In 1391 for example, a case is committed to the Chancellor so that there should be done 'what right and reason and good faith and good conscience require'.[42] In giving the king Reason and Conscience as his chief advisors in the Prologue, Langland is setting the scene for the king's direct judgment according to the principles of equity in *Passus* IV.

This could be the reason why Langland removed from the C-text Prologue all those passages which suggested that the king should rule according to law or Parliament. When a king judged through his prerogative courts he acted as an absolute monarch. Indeed contemporary Parliaments treated the development of equity as a most suspicious growth of the king's political power. But as I shall now show, Langland believed that only such a development could counteract the threat which Lady Meed had brought to the *Visio* kingdom – which is England. It is to overcome Meed that Langland created a king who is not only genuinely guided by Reason and Conscience, but also an absolute monarch. Pragmatic rather than idealistic, he has cut his political theory according to England's lawless and unhappy cloth.

II

LADY MEED: THE THREAT TO AUTHORITY

Passus II-IV compose the only complete dramatic sequence in *Piers Plowman* which centres on the theme of government. They describe what threatens social justice and the king's authority in a kingdom very like Langland's England. This threat is first embodied (*Passus* II-III) in Lady Meed and her retinue, and this chapter will establish what she represents in contemporary life. The next chapter will describe her association with Wrong, and show how the *Visio* king — though not Langland's own king — overcomes them both through asserting his absolute power (*Passus* IV). In doing so he not only controls a rival power, but prevents it from infiltrating his own Council and ousting the Reason and Conscience which justify his own authority.

1. Who is Lady Meed?

Lady Meed is introduced as the enemy of Truth and Holy Church, and most critics interpret her primarily as a moral threat. To Robertson and Huppé she is descended from Antichrist and the Whore of Babylon, who tempt men to choose the earthly rather than the heavenly City. To Mitchell she is morally ambiguous, but her indiscriminate generosity corrupts others. To Dawson she is 'the power of the purse', and Yunck has documented the long line of 'venality satire' from which such a personification is descended.[1] He relates this tradition to the changing economic conditions of the later Middle Ages, when services which had supposedly once been done for love (such as dispensing the Sacraments) were only to be had for money. The followers of Lady Meed in *Piers Plowman* are thus committing a moral offence akin to simony, in that they are selling the Gifts of the

24

Holy Spirit, their learning, their professional skill, their official or sacramental power.

These analyses illumine Langland's ethical concerns, but they do not explain precisely what he was attacking in his own society. Why is Meed a noblewoman, the kinswoman of the king, if she represents only a moral threat? Why does her own defence of her activities to Conscience in *Passus* III have so much to do with war? Why does she allow into her retinue more secular and legal officials than members of the Church?

Yunck's analysis of venality satire concentrated on how money corrupts the soul, but Langland's Lady Meed belongs equally to the late medieval tradition of venality satire which was concerned with the way that the power and influence which money can bring were beginning to harm society. Poems such as *The Simonie* (c.1327) and *Wynnere and Wastoure* (mid-fourteenth century) for example, attack not only the pride and extravagance of Churchmen, but also the proud and oppressive retinues of great lords, who owned so much of the country's wealth.[2] Poems written after *Piers Plowman* even develop the character of Lady Meed herself into a personification of the evil noble. A fifteenth-century poet describes the Civil Wars as a time when the well-dressed man dealt in 'murdre . . . usure and rapyne', and he blames all such iniquity on 'the mayde Mede'.[3] In another poem 'Mede' appears as the evil noble who counsels the king, and boasts:

> My flateryng, glosyng, not me harmes.
> I gete loue, *and* moche richesse.[4]

This 'Mede' is like 'Mum' in *Mum and the Sothsegger*, the counsellor who sucks up the king's wealth and then shows him how to wring more from his poor commons. Since late medieval poets were concentrating so much satire on the lawless noble and evil counsellor, and even calling such men 'Meed', it is probable that Langland's own readers would have found Lady Meed's nobility and her effect on the king, as significant as her association with Simony and Civil.

What the nobility had on offer was not the Gifts of the Holy Spirit but money and power. They had discovered an easy way to use and increase that power during the Hundred Years' War with France. From 1341 the lords were encouraged to sign 'indentures' with the king, contracting to find, equip, pay and command a certain number of soldiers, for which they would receive sufficient money from the king (Lady Meed seems to claim credit for this system in *Passus* III).[5] Obviously the presence of such a company of soldiers wearing his livery increased a lord's prestige, and it became increasingly common for him to retain them during peace-time on his own account. He would pay them an annuity and call on their services when required. These 'retainers' composed a loose and rather undisciplined addition to the normal households of lords in the later fourteenth and fifteenth centuries. Modern historians often refer to this phenomenon as 'bastard feudalism' because it is 'far removed indeed from the atmosphere of responsibility, loyalty and faith which had characterized the relationship of lord and vassal in the earlier Middle Ages.'[6]

Gradually the lords also began to offer fees and liveries to 'any available neighbour or tenant'[7] if he would only appear on ceremonial occasions, and generally promote his patron's interests in everyday life. Localities thus became divided between different allegiances, and the wishes of the local lord could easily be the most important consideration in any dispute. The members of the professions and the administrative officers acting in his locality found it either useful or unavoidable to ally themselves with him. Indeed this nobleman was often responsible for getting them their positions: for nominating local knights to be Justices of the Peace and sheriffs, for securing royal Justices their Commissions of the Peace, for providing valuable livings for his clerks, for interceding on behalf of each to the king or his courtiers. In return he expected his retainers to be taxed lightly, or to be granted lands in preference over others, or, most important, to protect them from the full force of the law if they got into trouble. It was this 'maintenance-at-law' which made the late medieval retinues so dangerous to social justice, for they prevented the king's law from being effective in certain localities. Moreover the very fact that involvement in such allegiances became so general, made it very difficult to stop. As Winfield wrote in his history of maintenance:

> the Statute-book and Parliament Rolls from [Edward III's] reign to the middle of the Tudor dynasty are long registers of constant failures to scotch evils of this kind. . . . At one moment the King, his Council, and Parliament are giving remedies against these offences. At the next, he and they are committing them. The judges, the sheriffs, the Justices of the Peace, the clergy were no better.[8]

Indeed at the top of the chain of patronage was the king himself, whose courtiers and trusted advisors had composed a kind of retinue long before Richard II formally issued the livery of the White Hart in 1390. The numerous prizes the king had to bestow were invariably suspected of attracting unsuitable counsellors, and there was more evidence than usual for such suspicions in the period when Langland was writing − the last decade of Edward III's reign and the first decade of Richard II's. And like the retainers of the nobility, these courtiers were accused not only of mercenariness, but of interference with the law.[9]

26

It is therefore necessary to take the allegory of Lady Meed and her retinue more literally than has hitherto been done. Langland's readers would surely have recognised her not only as a personification of corrupt reward, but as a lifelike example of the kind of person who used such reward in order to sustain and protect an unscrupulous retinue, and so increase her own power. (In rather the same way, the characters described in *Passus* VI are not only allegorisations of Deadly Sins but representatives of typical sinners; this is Langland's characteristic method of allegory.) Indeed, Meed uses not only reward but all her noble attributes — charm, influence, high birth — to undermine the law and win political power at the king's court. She even promises to win the king a retinue to defeat his enemies in war and surround him with grateful courtiers in peace-time. Langland can then be placed among those late medieval poets who attacked the power of the nobility in the localities and at court, and begged the king to find truthful advisors and so purge his kingdom.

2. The composition of Meed's retinue

Lady Meed first appears in *Piers Plowman* dressed for her marriage to False, and surrounded by the enormous retinue she has summoned for the ceremony. This must have suggested to Langland's audience the lavish display of a great noble as well as the pervasive power of the purse:

> Al þe riche retenaunce þat rotheth hem o fals lyuynge
> Were beden to þe bridale a bothe half þe contre,
> Of many manere men þat of Mede kynne were,
> Of knyghtes, of clerkes, of other comune peple,
> As sysores, sompnores, shyryues and here clerkes,
> Bydels and bailifs and brokeres of chaffares,
> Vorgoers and vitalers and voketes of the Arches,
> Y kan nouȝt rykene þe route þat ran aboute Mede.

C.II.55-62

Meed's acceptance of 'þe meene and þe riche' (B.II.56) into her train is only slightly less discriminating than the medieval lord's. The livery roll of Edward Countenay, Earl of Devonshire (who, as will be seen, is almost a model for Langland's Meed) includes for 1384-5 five male kinsmen, seven knights, forty esquires, fifty-two yeomen (including estates officials like bailiffs), eight parsons and fourteen men of law.[10] Lady Meed can also boast other groups, such as the 'vorgoers and vitalers' (61) or 'purveyors' who might provision a great household. But her retinue is not restricted to those who wear her livery or who attend her marriage, and over the next two *Passus* we discover just how many officials of the secular administration and courts are of her allegiance. (I do not include the clerical officials and lawyers whose corruption does not interfere with the government of the *kingdom*, which is my chief concern, though it does of course upset the government of the *Church*.) These followers misuse their offices not only by taking bribes, but by manipulating the influence which their association with a great noble gave them.

At this point, Meed is in the country, and her retinue is largely composed of men who share the responsibility for local government: knights, sheriffs with their under-officers, the beadles and bailiffs, and 'sisors' or jurymen. Langland does not have much further to say about the corruption of knights, although Parliament complained more than once that the local allegiances of Justices of the Peace (chosen from among knights) affected their impartiality and even made them 'commonly maintainers of evil-doers'.[11]

Langland has more to say about the sheriffs and their officers, for Conscience will tell the king in the next *Passus* that they would be ruined without her:

> 'Shyreues of shyres were shent yf she nere,
> For she doth men lesen here lond and here lyf bothe.
> She lat passe prisones, paieth for hem ofte,
> And gyueth the gayler gold and grotes togederes
> To vnfetere the fals and fle wher hym lyketh;
> And taketh treuthe by the top and teieth hym faste
> And hangeth hym for hatrede þat harmede nere.'

C.III.171-7

Although sheriffs were the king's chief representatives in the counties, it was very difficult for them to be impartial, partly because they were supposed to pay their own wages out of the fines, taxes and fees they collected, and partly because they probably owed their position to the patronage of some great local lord. As Langland implies, they had considerable powers over personal freedom: they issued the writs in civil cases; they apprehended suspects in criminal cases; and they kept the prisons. It was often claimed that they imprisoned men falsely, either in order to exact heavy fines for their release, or to suit the purposes of their patron.[12] It was even possible to get a man 'hanged for hatred', as can be seen from the fact that one could apply for bail on the grounds that one had been indicted 'from spite and malice'.[13] So commonly were gaolers bribed by escaping prisoners, that they or the sheriff were always fined when anybody escaped from custody, and occasionally special commissions were sent into particular areas to find out why so many prisoners were being allowed to 'fle wher hym lyketh' (175). When a knight called Thomas Oughtred was actually imprisoned for highway robbery by an unusually honest Sheriff of York in 1361, he was so appalled that the sheriff had not accepted his 'gold and grotes' (474) that he got him dismissed in disgrace![14]

The easiest way for a sheriff to help his local patron when he or his retainers got into trouble was however to appoint a sympathetic jury to try them. It was because jurors found it practically impossible to resist local pressures which made them the weakness rather than the strength of the judicial system. 'Sisors' (members of an 'assize', or jury in a civil action) are in fact the most frequently mentioned members of Meed's secular retinue, and even remain with her after her disgrace (C.IV.162).[15] Jurors were not asked for their opinion of the case, but for their knowledge of the facts, which they could not always have had. Since they were generally humble men they would not easily resist the version of the facts presented to them by a representative of the lord on whom they were dependent — as the sheriff or bailiff who chose them would have ensured. Some sheriffs even employed the same jurors again and again, giving them an almost professional position as 'questmongers', like the

Tomme Two-tonge, ateynt at vch enqueste

mentioned in C.XXII.162.[16] It is clear from their inclusion in Meed's retinue that Langland believed most sisors to be willing perjurers. ·

Indeed the ride which False and Favel plan to make to Westminster on sisors' backs (C.II.179-180) almost literally reflects the kind of precautions which a false but wealthy individual could take to ensure he was never bested at law. In 1391 the Abbot of Osyth complained that no-one could stop the maintenance of his neighbour John Rockell, because:

> so many Ministers, Officers, Bailiffs and ... common jurors are of his livery or allegiance, that ... Johan ... Rockell does not care what he does, for he fears no punishment ... from the Common Law. [And indeed when he goes before the courts in Westminster] he brings with him an entire jury, ... so as to accomplish his purposes easily.[17]

Meed herself rides on a sheriff (177) indicating perhaps that when such officials came to London, for example as members of Parliament, they could be expected to forward only the interests of their friends in the shires, as the Commons complained in 1371.[18] The relationship between Meed and local officials and jurymen is of benefit to both sides.

If Meed's retinue is built in the localities, like that of many a provincial lord, she herself needs to use it in the capital. When she arrives in London she has apparently lost the protection of the knights, sheriffs and the like, and at once sets about surrounding herself with judges and borough officials. The judges even come to welcome her, expecting that like most great nobles she would find it advantageous to retain one permanently. (This practice was repeatedly forbidden, but the king did not pay his judges enough to persuade them to stop finding additional employers.)[19]

Conscience is to complain also to the king in *Passus* III of the partiality of judges and arbitrators:

> 'By Iesu! with here ieweles the iustices she shendeth; ...
> And leet þe lawe as here luste and louedayes maketh.
> Thorw which loueday is loste þat Leute myhte wynne — ...
> Lawe is so lordliche and loth to make eny ende.'
>
> <div align="right">C.III.192-8 <i>passim.</i></div>

All of law is under Meed's, rather than 'leute's' control partly because justice moved through such tortuous channels.[20] These would inevitably favour the richest suitor, who could ask for 'essoins' (deferments) or buy a *supersedeas* (which suspended the case altogether) until his opponent sought an out-of-court settlement at a 'loveday'. These were usually held at this period by a local lord of the kind typified by Lady Meed herself, and in consequence favoured the richer suitor quite as much as the courts. A Middle English poem on lovedays expects from them only more maintenance-at-law:

> for þis man is my frend
> I wile mayntene þis man & al his matere als.[21]

What was needed was either legal reform, or a more effective alternative to the Common Law than lovedays provided. We will see later how the king restores 'leute'.

If Meed collects judges around her in order to help her own case, she also collects some borough officials in order to make life in London easier for her friends and retainers. These are the dishonest retainers, whose allegiance to Meed must be interpreted more in terms of their general dishonesty than a participation in bastard feudalism. Once again it is influence and bribery which makes law ineffective, and allows the poor to be harmed by the unscrupulous (C.III.77-89). The mayor even makes profitable allegiances, quite in the manner of Lady Meed herself, with certain rather questionable traders:

> Forthy mayres þat maketh fre men, me thynketh þat ʒe ouhten
> For to spyre and to aspye, for eny speche of suluer
> What maner muster oþer marchandise he vsed
> Ar he were vnderfonge fre and felawe in ʒoure rolles.
> Hit is nat seemely for sothe in citee or in borw-toun

That vsurers oþer regraters, for enys-kynes ʒeftes,
Be yfranchised for a fre man and haue a fals name.

C.III.108-114

The inhabitants of London who had not been born citizens with the 'freedom of the city' could purchase that privilege if they had obtained the consent of the Common Council of the City, together with the consent of the guild which governed the craft or 'muster' (110) they wished to follow. It became increasingly common in the later fourteenth century for potential citizens to give a 'fals name' (114) for the trade they wished to join, either in order to pay less for enfranchisement, or in order to disguise their true profession. 'Mercers' say they are 'Haberdasheres'; a Lombard broker (and so probably a usurer) pays heavily to become a freeman Mercer.[22] Another kind of 'name changing' occured in 1378. The mayor, Nicholas Brembre, was discovered to have sold the freedom on his own authority to an alien who changed his name from 'Hosyer' to 'Curteys' — presumably because he was so notorious under his own name.[23] This may have been the very case which prompted Langland's allusion. What makes him so angry is, as always, that officials like the mayor have the complete responsibility for enforcing justice; if they are corrupt, then the poor are unprotected from evil-doers.

It is clear then that Meed and her retinue present a serious threat to the king's government. She corrupts officials in the localities and the capital, and her 'maintenance-at-law' prevents local, central, and borough courts from administering justice impartially. Conscience rejects her hand in marriage for these reasons, but it will not be until *Passus* IV, discussed in the next Chapter, that the king will turn against her and try to restore social justice to his kingdom by imprisoning her.

What is at first surprising is that she is brought to Westminster not because she has corrupted local law and government, but because she has attempted to marry without the king's leave. What does this mean, either in the allegorical logic of the poem, or in real medieval life? If Meed represents a great noblewoman, why should she need the king's permission to marry? If her retinue is so pernicious, why does the king want to establish her in his court by marrying her to one of his courtiers? And what does all this contribute to Langland's theme of government?

3. Meed's marriages

The allegory of Meed's marriages, like that of her person and retinues, has usually been interpreted in general moral terms. Yunck for example saw her proposed union with False as the corruption of the principle of reward in a money-economy, and the king's alternative of marriage to Conscience as an attempt to reward goodness with material benefit.[24] There is nothing wrong with such an interpretation, but it is imprecise, because it does not take account of the real-life situations on which the allegory is modelled. Since these concern a king's dealings with his more powerful subjects, they give a political basis to the allegory which involves a warning for Langland's own king. For like other late medieval venality satirists, Langland demonstrates that the great nobles with their retinues are at their most dangerous in the councils of the king.

From a social point of view the situation that confronts Will at the beginning of *Passus* II seems to be the attempted 'disparagement' of Meed, that is, an attempt to marry her to someone of much lower status.[25] Holy Church may have called Meed a bastard (C.II. 24), but Theology points out that she is the daughter of Amendes, and a relation of the king, and should not be thrown away on False Faithless:

> 'Fals is faythles, the fende is his syre,
> And as a bastard ybore byȝete was he neuere.
> And Mede is moylore and mayden of gode;
> A myhte kusse the kyng as for his kynneswomman.'

C.II.143-6

The bride and groom are ready to fall in with this project in order to get the '*maritagium*' or marriage-settlement promised by Meed's father. This is drawn up in so exact a parody of a real 'feoffment' or gift of land, as to cast a disturbing light on genuine *maritagia* (C.II. 79-115). This grotesque allegory of a marriage-gift of the Deadly Sins and Hell, is locked into the real-life world of mercenary matches – as for example

> the union of John Woodville aged about twenty with Katherine Neville, widow of . . . [the] Duke of Norfolk, a lady well over sixty, which made a chronicler write indignantly of *maritagium diabolicum*.[26]

On one level then this marriage represents the 'disparagement' of the principle of reward in medieval England when it is allied – as in such mercenary marriages – with Falsity. In more general social terms, a disparaging union between Meed and False Faithless suggests that very bastardisation of the principles of 'responsibility, loyalty and faith' practised by all who allied themselves to great lords as wealthy and unscrupulous as Lady Meed herself.

Whereas on a moral level the marriage angers Truth, on a political level it angers the king. Theology warns the bride and groom that they may be breaking the law, and as if recognising the truth of this they meekly pack up and go to London:

> 'ther lawe may declare
> Where matrymonye may be of Mede and of Falshede'
>
> C.II.148-9

Now disparagement was not illegal unless either party was a 'ward', an orphan under protection, and Meed is not an orphan; indeed her father helped promote the match (II.43, 65). Even if she were, the king seems to over-react. He sends out an order to 'hang those wretches' (206-7), a punishment more appropriate to the criminal offence of 'ravishment' (abducting an heiress) than to the civil one of disparagement.[27] Why is the law or the king involved at all?

The king's involvement can only be explained in terms of the information that Meed is his kinswoman (C.II.146) and so presumably, heiress to one of his tenancies-in-chief. For feudal law insisted that

> Women that hold of the King in Chief any Inheritance, of whatsoever Age they be, shall . . . not marry themselves without the King's Licence; and if they do, their Lands and Tenements shall be taken . . . into the King's Hands, until they have satisfied at the King's Will.[28]

This is why in *Passus* III the king reproaches Meed because she

> wilned to be wedded withouten his leue   C.III.131

By letting the allegory imply that the king is Meed's lawful protector, Langland is demonstrating the king's responsibility over his nobles and their wealth. For he, the Caesar of England, should ensure that the 'moneye of þis molde' (C.I.42) is used to service a balanced and legal state, and not appropriated by a few families to build up their own power and spheres of influence. He must intervene in Meed's marriage to protect his own power, as well as the justice and peace of the kingdom.

The obvious solution to the problem of the over-powerful noble was to enlist his support and give him a position of responsibility at court. This must be partly what the *Visio* king has in mind when he offers Meed his favourite courtier, Conscience, as bridegroom. The plan has the additional advantage of rewarding Conscience with a valuable marriage. It was indeed largely through granting such benefits as churches, offices, lands, wardships (the income from a ward's lands) and marriages (the chance to marry or to sell the marriage of an heir or heiress) that the medieval king rewarded loyalty and built up his own political position.[29] It was for this very reason that the king's councillors could be accused of mercenariness or of impoverishing the realm, by their rivals or opponents. Conscience himself would certainly be open to such suspicions if he accepted Meed in marriage, and in any case she would be a dangerous figure to have permanently at court. Consequently when Conscience rejects Meed he calls into question the whole principle that nobles and others should be attracted to the court by the chance that they would receive there power, influence and wealth.

To illustrate this Conscience points to two situations — one past, one present — in which the king's attention to mercenary councillors or courtiers threatened to lose him the general love of his subjects. First he refers to the king's father:

> '3oure fader she afelde, Fals and she togederes'.   C.III.162

Readers of the B or C-texts would most likely identify '3oure fader' not with Adam (as the A-text indicates, A.III.114, *cp.* B.III.127) but with Edward III, Richard II's grandfather, and Meed with Alice Perrers, his mistress from the 1360s. Edward allowed her and a circle of courtiers to remove thousands of pounds from the royal resources and this, as the contemporary literature and Parliament Rolls indicate, lost him much of his popularity in the final years of his reign.[30] At this point, Conscience seems to suspect his king of wanting Meed to marry a courtier so that she, like Alice Perrers, would be a constant figure at court (Meed herself will indicate her advantages as a counsellor later in the *Passus*).

In the C-text Conscience also warns his king that just such a situation has arisen again now. The *Visio* king, he says (and here Langland must be addressing his own king, Richard II), has nearly lost the true loyalty of his subjects by taking the advice of Lady Meed or of the kind of courtiers she attracts:

> 'Ther ne is cite vnder sonne ne noon so ryche reume
> Ther she is alowed and ylet by þat laste shal eny while
> Withouten werre oþer wo oþer wickede lawes
> And custumes of coueytise þe comune to destruye.
> Vnsittyng soffraunce, here suster, and heresulue
> Han almest mad, but Marye the helpe,
> That no lond ne loueth the and 3ut leeste thyn owene.'
>
> C.III.203-9

These lines criticise the present government more openly than anything else in the poem, and since they occur only in the C-text they probably refer to the period between 1378 and 1387 when that text was probably written.

Before 1382 Richard II was treated as a minor and it was the Continual Councils, which more or less mismanaged the government, which should have been blamed for Meed's presence at court. However, from the first, Richard showed all too much 'soffraunce' (207) towards greedy courtiers. Parliament was not slow to complain that courtiers were sapping the king of his real income by demanding innumerable gifts, grants, and lands, and then subjecting the 'commune' (206) to the burdensome Poll Taxes.[31] These unprecedented taxes might well have been described as 'wickede lawes' (205), but then so could have many of the methods which the courtiers used to get money. From 1379 onwards the Commons persistently complained that illegal means were being used to dispossess the tenants of royal lands in order to grant them to others. In 1379 the Commons also exposed the practice of selling demands for forced loans to courtiers, who could then fill in the name of anyone they pleased on the blank cover above the mark of the Privy Seal, and demand money from him.[32] Such men could fairly be described as caring only for Meed; indeed they acted as one would expect Lady Meed herself to act.

If Langland was writing these lines after 1382, Conscience's assertion that 'no lond ne loueth the' makes even more sense when applied to the reigning king. In that year Richard dismissed the Chancellor, who had tried to control his generosity, and until Parliament took over the government again in 1386, he might fairly have been blamed for the 'custumes of coueytise' practised at court. Things deteriorated so much that in 1386 his uncle the Duke of Gloucester threatened him with the fate of Edward II:

Heavy taxation was producing a nation of paupers; evil counsellors were at the root of its miseries, let the king remember that 'by ancient statute and recent precedent' they have a remedy. A king who is guided by evil counsel, who withdraws himself from his people, neglects to maintain their laws, and is governed only by his own capricious impulses, can be removed from the throne ... The great and famous realm of England ... is now desolate and divided.[33]

Thus from the beginning of his realm until 1386 Richard II could have been accused with increasing force of inappropriate indulgence, of covetous customs, and even of wicked laws and the destruction of the commons, so that no land loved him, and particularly not his own. At this point in the poem it seems that neither England nor the *Visio* kingdom will be well governed until the king ceases to reward his counsellors with Meed, and so ceases to attract those whose greed or unscrupulous methods suggest Meed herself. Instead he should accept only the disinterested advice of Conscience, and drive Meed away for ever.

Meed however now begins to defend herself both as the kind of prize who attracts courtiers, and as a courtier in her own right (C.III. 220-282). She tells the king that, far from harming him, or attracting evil followers to him, she can buy him a retinue which will win him both love and respect:

> 'Hit bycometh for a kyng þat shal kepe a reume
> To ʒeue men mede þat meekliche hym serueth,
> To aliens and to alle men, to honoure hem with ʒeftes;
> Mede maketh hym be byloued and for a man yholde.'

C.III.263-7

This is as it were a summary of her defence; before she makes this more general claim she has argued that the retinues she has already supplied have won the king's wars (C.III.233-263). She seems here to be speaking as the creator of the indentured army, of which the late medieval retinues were a by-product. Indentured soldiers genuinely did fight for Meed — for their good wages, their share in captured goods and ransoms, and even for the land their captain could be granted.[34] Meed's words must have recalled the sense of partnership in a successful enterprise enjoyed by those fighting the early campaigns of the Hundred Years' War:

> 'The leste ladde þat longeth with hym [the king], be þe londe ywonne,
> Loketh aftur lordschipe or oþer large mede
> Wherby he may as a man for eueremore lyue aftur.
> And þat is þe kynde of a kyng þat conquereth on his enemys,
> To helpe heyliche alle his oste or elles graunte
> Al þat his men may wynne, do therwith here beste.'

C.III.247-252

Again Meed is suggesting the value of living up to expectations (263, 250), of being accounted 'a man' (267, 249). And it was true that many knights made fortunes in France. Sir Robert Knollys was given

> 'forty castles' in the valley of the Loire, the lands of Doreval and Rouge in Brittany, with their reputed rental of two thousand *livres* . . .[35]

War was also profitable for the 'leste ladde' (247) in a successful army. Froissart described how at Barfleur 'there was found so much riches that the boys and villains of the host set nothing by good furred gowns'. It is not surprising that he commented elsewhere that the English are 'covetous and envious . . . above measure of other men's wealth'.[36] Lady Meed did marshall the great indentured armies of Edward III.

Meed contrasts her success with Conscience's cowardice. His counsel, we are to understand, was for peace:

> 'Ac thow thysulue sothly, ho hit segge durst,
> Hast arwed many hardy man þat hadde wille to fyhte,
> To berne and to bruttene, to bete adoun strenghtes. . .

'Caytifliche thow, Consience, conseiledest þe kyng to leten
In his enemyes handes his heritage of Fraunce.'

C.III.235-7, 241-2

The violence of this description of medieval warfare, particularly its implication of the 'dampnum'[37] or march of devastation, which was so effective in France, leaves us in no doubt that Langland was with Conscience in this matter. Such wholesale methods were only legitimate in a 'public' war, fought by a Prince to redress an injury, but Edward III's claim to have a 'heritage of Fraunce' (242) sounds particularly spurious when spoken by Meed.[38] If Conscience wants the king to renounce his heritage, then he wants him to renounce the right to wage further public war in France. In the B-text Meed associates Conscience with the Treaty of Bretigny of 1360, when Edward did — for a time — renounce his claim, in return for considerable territory and three million gold crowns. Meed enjoys baiting Conscience for having robbed the poor men of France, who paid the first down payment at Calais in October (B.III.195-208).[39] By associating Conscience with peace policies and Meed with the war, Langland is not only taking the unusual line of discrediting the war as a greedy and unscrupulous affair.[40] He is also descrediting the kind of policy which Meed and her bought retinue would advocate at court.

The king however seems to be attracted by Meed's promises of glory and love:

Quod þe kyng to Consience, 'By Crist, as me thynketh,
Mede is worthy, me thynketh, þe maistrye to haue.'

C.III.283-4

Conscience therefore tries to explain to the king precisely what Meed is. He does this first by distinguishing between two kinds of reward, in a passage I shall discuss at the beginning of the last chapter (pp. 56-57). He then returns more specifically to the subject of royal retinues, and explains that a wise king will not use gifts as an incentive for loyalty (as Meed does), but as a reward for proven loyalty which can be withdrawn if the loyalty fails:

'And thow the kyng of his cortesye, cayser or pope,
Ʒeue lond or lordschipe oþer large ʒeftes
To here lele and to lege, loue ys the cause,
And yf the lele and lege be luyther men aftur
Bothe kyng and cayser and þe crouned pope
May desalowe that thei dede and dowe þerwith another . . .
Noyther eny of here ayres hardy to claymen

C.III.314-9, 321

This is not the first, and will not be the last time in the poem that Langland's precise knowledge of treason and its penalties helps him to define the loyalty due from all to their king, their God, their own Consciences. Treason was a breach of the subject's first duty: his allegiance to his ruler, his 'Kyng . . . , cayser, or pope' (314, 318). It was punished not only by drawing and hanging the traitor, but by returning all his lands to the king as 'escheat', since the king ultimately owned all land, and only as it were 'leased' it to his tenants and their vassals on the condition of their loyalty. What Bracton had said in the early thirteenth century remained true at least in theory in Langland's day:

> [the traitor] shall suffer the exteme penalty, with torture . . . the loss of all his goods, and the perpetual disherison of his heirs . . . If they are some-times admitted to the succession it will be more as a matter of grace than of right.[41]

Conscience reinforces his point with the Biblical examples of Solomon and Saul (C.III.323-331, 406-435), who both lost their kingdoms for disobedience to their heavenly King. The message for the *Visio* king is clear enough; he has no need to buy loyalty with Meed, for he can expect it as of right and law. His best counsellors will serve him with no thought of reward, and any property he might give them should be thought of only as a wage for their continuing service. If however he prefers to trust Meed's counsel, then there is a warning for him in the fates of Solomon and Saul.

All in all it seems that retinues bought through Meed can only harm the government of England. If Conscience is to be believed, then the retinues of local lords stifle legal and administrative impartiality in the provinces, in the central courts, and in the boroughs. If the king tries to create a court party in the same way, he can say farewell to justice in peace or war. The reader may be convinced of this, but the *Visio* king is not. He still expects a reconciliation between Meed and Conscience (C.IV.1-3). Accordingly, Langland brings Peace into the court to demonstrate finally how the country has been given over to crime and oppression by the king's failure to control the power of his nobles, and by his own compromises with Meed. And thereby Meed will be shown in her true colours, as a councillor who puts her own and her friends' interests far above the sufferings of the king's poor commons.

III

THE TRIUMPH OF AUTHORITY

The effect of *Passus* II and III has been to convince the reader of *Piers Plowman* that the *Visio* kingdom – England – has been ill-governed. Because of the king's own tolerance of Lady Meed, she and others like her have been allowed to make their own law in the provinces, and even in the capital itself.

The result of this governmental weakness in Langland's England was widespread oppression and crime. Parliament clearly recognised that law and order were deteriorating, and even interpreted the Peasants' Revolt of 1381 partly as a protest against:

> the grevious oppressions committed in the country by the outrageous numbers of men who take up and maintain quarrels, and are as Kings in the country, so that right and law are almost set at nothing.[1]

Not only did the retainers themselves flout the law, but some criminal bands actually joined the allegiance (and filled the coffers) of particularly influential lords. The Folville gang of brothers (whom Langland mentions approvingly in *Passus* XXI. 247!), operating in the first half of the century, escaped punishment principally because they were the sons of one knight and wore the livery of another. Their chief patron, Sir Robert Tuchet (or Touchet) also 'maintained' the Coterel gang – and no doubt shared the profits of both.[2] When such gangs were brought to the courts they escaped conviction by befriending or intimidating the court officials and the jury. In 1388, for example, John Biere of Bodmin, whose servants had been attacked and whose merchandise had been stolen, challenged the king with the responsibility of maintaining his peace. He blamed a gang who

> of their covin gathered to themselves many other maintainers and disturbers of the King's peace, Inasmuch that they would not be justified by the Sheriff of the County against their will, nor will they at any time, unless our lord the King betakes himself against them seriously.[3]

Lady Meed's maintenance-at-law has thus prepared the way for the oppression and the crimes of Wrong. The *Visio* King had remained unconvinced by Conscience's attack on Meed in *Passus* III, but he will have to believe the evidence of his own eyes in *Passus* IV, where she protects Wrong in his own court. Conscience might also have told him that Wrong would never have got such assurance if Meed had not protected him in every lesser court in the land. It is high time for the king to 'betake himself against them seriously'.

1. The petition of Peace

The trial towards which *Passus* II and III have been leading takes place at C.IV.42-196, (B.IV.44-195). It does not concern the attempted marriage of Meed to False, which the king seems to have forgiven (C.III.138), but the petition of one 'Peace' against the crimes of 'Wrong'. It takes place in a 'parlement' (C.IV.45) where the King and Conscience preside, together with a new counsellor, Reason, who has just arrived but soon takes the initiative. He has a right to do so, for as I explained in the first Chapter, Reason was both a higher faculty of the soul than Conscience, and was associated with the Natural Law which validated the laws of a kingdom.[4]

It is important to decide whether this is simply an idealised abstraction of government, or whether it is modelled on anything specific in Langland's England. In the first place, what does this 'parlement' (C.IV.45) or 'conseyl' (C.III.127) represent? Taking all three texts into account — as it is unlikely that Langland meant to represent different assemblies in each — we notice the presence of 'clerkus . . . and Erlis' (B.IV.189) and lawyers (C.IV.67), besides the king's Privy Council of advisors: Reason and Conscience. In the C-text Reason is finally given the key position of Chancellor, and Conscience is made Chief Justice (C.IV.185-6). The Commons are absent (particularly if C.IV.176-7 refers to them), but then one would not expect their presence at any Parliamentary trial.

The largest assembly that the passage could therefore describe would be a meeting of the House of Lords sitting as a court, as 'Fleta' rather vaguely defined it in about 1290:

> . . . the king has his court in his council in his parliaments, in the presence of prelates, earls, barons, nobles and other learned men, where judicial doubts are determined, and new remedies are established for new wrongs, and justice is done to every one according to his deserts.[5]

Langland's assembly is probably not a meeting of this full Parliament, for reasons that will become apparent. The king could however have his 'court in his council' in a more precise sense in Langland's day, and such meetings were also called 'Parliaments'. These were meetings of the Privy Council, which was then beginning to sit sometimes as a court, as is described in one case in 1366:

> Proceedings in a parliament holden at Westminster ... and before the council ... to wit the chancellor, treasurer, justices, and other wise men assembled in the Star Chamber.[6]

The Chancellor and Chief Justices would more naturally preside at such a court than in Parliament, and this would correspond better to the position which Reason and Conscience occupy in *Passus* IV (in B.IV.45 they even sit 'on benche'). The Chancellor might also call the members of the Council to help him judge a case in Chancery, though as yet this was hardly a distinct court.

These courts of House of Lords, Council, and Council-in-Chancery were essentially different sittings of the same court, where the king dispensed justice on his own account and under his own prerogative. Even when he was not present himself, he would generally be consulted, and his consent was needed to validate their judgments. They provided a way for him to assert his 'absolute' authority over the law, as distinct from the power he generally wielded through an increasingly rigid legal and administrative system. His 'prerogative courts' in fact developed partly in response to the growing failure of law to control maintenance or stop the oppression of retainers. When a man failed to get justice through the courts, his only recourse was to petition the king. In the later fourteenth century the House of Lords, which traditionally received most petitions, began regularly to send those complaining of this kind of injustice to the Chancellor, who tried them with the Council sitting as a prerogative court either in Star Chamber or in Chancery. It is such a sitting that we watch in *Passus* IV.[7]

As I mentioned in the first chapter, a petitioner who had failed to obtain justice in the courts often asked the king not for law only, but for 'law and reason', or for 'right'. To put it in more modern terms, he needed the 'equity' which only the king could give, through his prerogative power to do *ad hoc* justice without recourse to normal legal procedures and precedents.[8] In 1381, for example, William and Margaret of Burcester complained to 'the very excellent lord the king and his very wise council' that

> they could not have right and reason in this matter because of the great maintenance at law of Sir Thomas de Hungreford [a local J.P.][9]

'Reason' was already an established name for the basic principles of justice, and by the fifteenth century, 'Conscience' was another, for Chancery was flatteringly referred to as the 'Court of Conscience'. In one case for example a petitioner asks that the defendant be called into

> the King's Chancery which is the Court of Conscience, there to answer thereto as reason and conscience demand.[10]

Langland's description of a petitioner bringing a complaint before a court where Reason and Conscience hold sway therefore reflects a genuine contemporary belief in the equitable jurisdiction of the king's prerogative courts. And in this we find an important justification for the absolutist views which Langland has expressed, particularly in the C-text Prologue. For if the king had no absolute power, he would have no prerogative to replace the law by his own equitable notion of justice.

But *is* Peace complaining of the failure of the law? What he actually says is that he has suffered certain oppressions and crimes at the hands of Wrong. Yet these are all actions forbidden under the Common Law, and had the law been working adequately Peace would not have needed to come to the king. Moreover, Wrong seems to have committed the oppressions and crimes which were typical of the unscrupulous retainers, relying as always on the protection which nobles like Lady Meed could offer against legal retribution. As one Wycliffite writer comments sourly, in words which echo many of Peace's complaints:

> also lordis many tymes done wrongis to pore men bi extorscions & vn-
> resonable mercymentis and vnresonable taxis, & taken pore mennus goodis
> & paien not þerfore but white stickis, & dispisen hem & manassen hem &
> sumtyme beten hem whanne þei axen here peye ... & summe lordis ...
> wolen to meyntene name of here lordischipe beten men of contre, &
> meyntenen oþer misdoeris þer-to, þouȝ men pursuen riȝt & reson in good
> manere ...[11]

To begin with Wrong's oppressions: these are mostly the high-handed requisitioning of goods that was associated with the 'purveyors' who found the supplies for royal and (at first) for noble households.

> 'Bothe my gees and my grys and my gras he taketh ...
> Ȝut is he bold for to borw and baddelyche he payeth
> For he borwed of me bayard, a brouhte hym hom neuere
> Ne no ferthyng therfore, for nouhte ich couthe plede ...
> And breketh vp my bernys dores and bereth awey my whete
> And taketh me but a tayle for ten quarteres otes' ...
>
> C.IV.49, 55-7, 60-1

The reeves of the manors of the Lord of Berkeley in Edward II's reign, for example, asked to be excused the loss of geese and ducks which had been taken by the purveyors of the Earl of Lancaster when travelling with the queen. These purveyors also 'broke open their barns and took wheat and corn'. Tallies were the subject of continual complaint, men of the West Country had, for example, to lobby the Black Prince in London before he would honour the debts incurred two years earlier in 1355.[12] Such nobles obviously allowed their retainers to oppress the poor.

In 1362 however the requisitioning of transport and provisions by ordinary retainers acting as provisors was made illegal, except when done for royal households. Even these purveyors were supposed to give 'ready payment in hand' for everything they took. Peace should have been able to get redress at Common Law for the illegal purveyance he has suffered, but since he clearly could not, he is following the procedure indicated in the 1362 statute: he is appealing to the Chancellor.[13]

More serious than Wrong's oppressions however are his crimes. He acts with all the boldness of a powerful neighbour, or his retainer, who has the law completely under his control. Peace explains:

> How Wrong wilfully hadde his wyf forleyn
> And how he raueschede Rose the ryche wydewe by nyhte
> And Margarete of here maydenhod as he mette here late . . .
> 'And a wayteth ful wel when y seluer take,
> What wey y wende wel ӡerne he aspyeth
> To robbe me or to ruyfle me yf y ryde softe . . .
> A meynteyneth his men to morthere myn hewes
> And forstalleth my fayres and fyhteth in my chepynges . . .
> And ӡut he manascheth me and myne and a lyth be my mayde,
> Y am nat hardy for hym vnnethe to loke.'
>
> C.IV.46-8, 52-4, 58-9, 63

Larceny, rape, murder and riding armed were all capital felonies: forcible entry, ravishment, forestalling, and maintenance were felonies that deserved imprisonment at least. A felony was an action committed 'against the king's peace', which would be prosecuted by the king if the wronged individual failed to do so. Felonies could only be heard in the king's own courts (the Central and the Assize courts).[14] Peace is therefore an allegorisation of the law and order for which the king was directly responsible. His presence before the king now demonstrates that the king has failed to protect the Peace through his own courts of Common Law.

Peace's petition is in fact very like the genuine petitions which complained of the breakdown of law and order, usually through maintenance, in Langland's day. Parallels can be found in Parliament, in the Council, and in the Council-in-Chancery. For example in 1378 the Commons in Parliament complained of criminal bands in much the same terms as Peace:

> many evil doers from the Counties of Chester & Lancaster . . . go wandering from day to day in order to kill your liegemen . . . and ravish their daughters and lead them away . . . [Others] in other Counties of the kingdom form confederacies and false alliances . . . and make great and evil extortions against the poor people of the country, & take their goods . . . & menace their lives, so that they dare not plead against them . . .[15]

Although the petitions against maintenance sent by individuals like Peace were also sometimes heard in the House of Lords,[16] they were generally sent on to the Chancellor to be heard before him and the Council, as I have already explained. Since the Council's early records are very fragmentary, it is in the Chancellor's own records that we find the closest parallels to Peace's petition, particularly since most of the early business of the council in Chancery were against violence and maintenance.[17]

In 1392 for example, William Hamlyn petitioned the Chancellor against John and Thomas Isbury, who, he said:

> lay in wait [for him], . . . beat him and wounded him . . . and did seize and carry off his goods and chattels, to wit, oxen, cows, corn and other goods . . . and further, . . . do continually threaten [him] from day to day to kill him, so that he dare not . . . sue them at Common Law for fear of death: Wherefore may it please your most gracious lordship to grant your said suppliant writs directed to the said John and Thomas [commanding them] to come before you in your place . . . considering, most gracious lord, that the said John and Thomas are so great in their country in kinsmen, alliances and friends, that the said suppliant cannot have right against them by any suit at Common law . . .[18]

In another case a petitioner complained that evil-doers have 'broke the houses and doors of his Vicarage'; in another that they:

> came to the market at Malton with twelve men arrayed with habergeons and palets, bows and arrows, swords and daggers, and very often they passed and re-passed through the said market, . . . and there they assaulted John de Navelton, esquire, and grievously menaced him . . .[19]

Peace was not alone in his lament that Wrong

> fyhteth in my chepynges,
> And breketh vp my bernys dores and bereth awey my whete.'
> C.IV. 57-60

All in all we may conclude that 'Wrong' was rampant in Langland's England, and that this was largely due to the protection nobles like Lady Meed offered him against the law, and that if all else failed, the best place to complain of him was in the Council of the king. To overcome them a force as powerful as they was needed, and it was only the king and his council who had the prerogative right and the power to bypass the corruptible processes of Common Law and bring them to justice.

2. The trial of Wrong

The climax of the Vision of Lady Meed and the King is the conviction first of Wrong, and then of Meed, who tries openly to protect him. These convictions depend on two things: the wisdom of the king in deciding, despite most of his counsellors, on what is just; and his absolute power to enforce that justice after the law has failed to do so. Had Langland believed in limiting the king by parliament or the law, he would not have exposed the fallibility of both. The *Visio* king's success in enforcing justice on his own authority could have been achieved in England through the prerogative courts which developed partly for that purpose. But in England the king was neither wise enough, nor absolutist enough, to make them work entirely in the service of equity.

The prerogative courts did have a chance to champion equity. They certainly employed more direct methods than the Common Law courts. Proceedings were begun not by a costly Latin writ or the indictment of a jury, but by a petition or 'bill' in the vernacular, often written by the petitioner himself. As Langland describes it:

'And thenne cam Pees into parlement and putte vp a bille   C.IV.45

The court then summoned the parties to appear before it, and it had the status and the machinery to force any defendant, however great, to obey the summons. When he was there the judges could cross-examine him, and then give judgement without recourse to a jury or to the complicated rules of Common Law. A corollary of this was that they could not impose punishment on life or limb, but had to be content with fines and imprisonment. The only appeal that could be made from such decisions was to the king's mercy.[20]

In practice one of the principle strengths of a prerogative court was its power to bring the malefactor to London, away from his local sphere of influence. This fact does not seem to have been sufficiently appreciated by Parliament, which was rather uncomfortably poised between being a prerogative and a Common Law Court, and which still used Common Law methods. For example it answered the Commons' complaint against the marauding bands from Chester and

Lancaster in 1378, by sending a Common Law Commission of Judges into the area. How these were offenders who had already shown their readiness to

> come before the justices in their sessions . . . with great force, so that the judges are much abashed, and do not dare to perform the Law.[21]

This kind of intimidation was all too common in the localities, but it was much more dangerous for a wrong-doer to try it in Westminster. That would insult 'the presence of the king and the whole parliament', as did the murder in 1398 of a suitor who was actually on his way through Fleet Street to have his case heard before the King's Council.[22] Wrong himself is not afraid of showing his teeth before the King's high Council, but he too will not get away with it here:

> ʒut Pees put forth his heued and hus panne blody
> 'Withouten gult, god wot, was gyue me this schathe'.
>
> C.IV.74-5

In order to prevent such intimidation, the Commission sent against the criminal bands in 1378 had special powers to 'intern' suspects without indictment or other process of law or option of bail or mainprise.[23] It was by using such methods that the *Visio* king had got Meed to Westminster (though her retinue, with the apparent exception of Wrong, escaped):

> 'Now by Crist', quod þe kyng 'and y cacche myhte
> Fals or Fauel or here felawe Lyare, . . .
> Shal neuere man on þis molde maynpryse þe leste,
> But ryht as þe lawe loketh lat falle on hem alle'
>
> C.II.204-5, 208-9

It was however difficult for Parliament to deny Common Law rights and processes, and it had to withdraw these powers from the Commission at its next session. When similar gangs were terrorising the Home Counties in 1399, it was the Council which sent a Commission to arrest all suspects and to imprison them without bail.[24] Parliament simply could not act wholeheartedly like a prerogative court. In denying Meed's followers the right to 'maynpryse' in *Passus* II the King is acting from his prerogative and against the normal methods of law and Parliament.

Since Wrong is present before the Council in *Passus* IV, we must understand that it has summoned him, probably by one of its own prerogative writs, such as the *subpoena*. These ignored many Common Law restrictions, and insisted that the accused come to London forthwith. They were inevitably more successful than Common Law Commissions in bringing suspects to trial. In 1391 for example, Edward Courtenay the Earl of Devonshire himself was charged under the Common Law with maintaining-at-law (by threatening the Justices) his retainer Robert Yeo. Yeo had actually murdered a man for daring to sue him. The Earl encouraged Yeo to disregard the Commission sent to arrest him, as he had disregarded all previous legal proceedings taken against him. But when the Council actually sent a polite version of the *subpoena* to the Earl himself, ordering him to come with Yeo before it, the Earl dared not disobey, even though he was himself a member of the King's Council, and (like Lady Meed) the King's kinsman.[25] The *Visio* king must have summoned Wrong to appear before him, for Wrong would never have allowed justice to be done to him at his home.

Once Wrong is before the Council, there seems to be little difficulty about establishing his guilt, for the Council did not have to ask a jury, but could decide the verdict themselves upon information, and on the advice of the judges (whom Conscience seems already to have joined as Chief Justice):

> Þe kyng knew that [Peace] saide soþ, for Conscience him tolde
> How Wrong was a wykked man and much wo wrouhte.'
>
> C.IV.64-5

The defendant in a case before Council was not even entitled to legal help. But Wrong manages to get some anyway:

> Tho was Wrong afered and Wisdom a souhte;
> On men of lawe Wrong lokede and largelyche hem profered
> And for to haue here helpe handy-dandy payde.
>
> C.IV.66-8

Taking Meed with them the lawyers[26] attempt to practise the maintenance-at-law which, as Langland hints, has protected Wrong from previous legal proceedings:

> Thorw Wrong and his werkes there was Mede yknowe,
> For Wysdom and Wyt tho wenton togyderes
> And token Mede with hem, mercy to wynne.
>
> C.IV.71-3

Meed is at last being shown for what she really is, the protector and the promoter of Wrong. He is as it were the leader of the criminal band who relies on her protection in exchange for her support. He is the retainer who feeds her power at the expense of the king's.

Unaffected by threats or bribes, the King determines to use the absolute authority of his crown to enforce justice in obedience to the laws of God:

> The kyng swor by Crist and by his croune bothe
> That Wrong for his werkes sholde wo tholye

And comaundede a constable to caste Wrong in yrones,
Ther he sholde nat in seuene ʒer see his feet ne handes

C.IV.79-82

But this decision is immediately opposed by those very factors which a limited monarch was bound to listen to: law, and Parliament. The normal legal practices of the Court of King's Council were unfortunately much more inclined to mercy than to justice, for all their prerogative powers. The councillors rarely even imposed the comparatively mild punishment of imprisonment on men who were often of the same class as they were, and whose maintenance might after all be no worse than their own. From the first they preferred to take sureties for good behaviour, to fine, or to encourage a settlement involving some form of compensation, rather than to humiliate the offender in prison. In fact imprisonment was generally only threatened in order to exact an enormous fine for the king's pardon. So it is that, at this crucial point, the lawyers indicate that legally Wrong is not bound to suffer, and the other councillors advise the king to be merciful. If the king were constrained to follow the guidance of law or Parliament, rather than his own Reason and Conscience, there would be no court in the land that upheld justice.

One councillor, in words full of double meaning, explains that it would be more profitable to ask 'maynprise' (bail or security) from Wrong than to punish him:

'Yf he amendes may do lat maynprise hym haue
And be borw for his bale and buggen hym bote
And amende þat is mysdo and euermore þe betere.'

C.IV.84-6

This councillor, like the lawyer Wit who takes up his argument (87-9) is hinting that the security ('maynprise', 'borw') which Wrong offers can be pocketed by the king as a palliative or cure ('bote') for the breach of his Peace.[27] This is a cue for Meed, who not only offers to stand surety ('wage') for Wrong, but also to pay compensation to Peace:

Then gan Mede to meken here and mercy she bisouhte
And profrede Pees a present al of puyre golde.
'Haue this, man, of me,' quod she, 'to amende thy scathe,
For y wol wage for Wrong he wol do so no mare'.

C.IV.90-93

Placing the offender upon security, and insisting that he compensate his victim, was indeed a normal and lucrative procedure in the court of the King's Council. It even increased the popularity of this court over Common Law courts, which had no power to order compensation or restoration of lost goods. In 1361 for example, the parson of Langay agreed to accept compensation from William Conyngsby, who had kidnapped and robbed him. The Council then dismissed Conyngsby without even demanding a fine, accepting instead security from a man they themselves trusted 'that William would henceforth conduct himself well and faithfully towards the King and his people'.[28] Even Peace can hardly be blamed for accepting compensation, and he asks the king to accept the security:

> Pitousliche Pees tho preyede the kyng
> To haue mercy on þat man that many tymes hym greuede
> 'For he haþ waged me wel as Wysdom hym tauhte
> And Mede hath made my mendes, y may no more asken,
> So alle myne claymes ben quyt by so þe kyng assente.'
>
> C.IV.94-8

In all these passages word-play is an indication of specious argument, and even Peace seems to be using 'wage' in a double sense. It means the gage or security offered by Meed that Wrong 'wol do so no mare' (93), and the payment he has 'earned' for agreeing to withdraw his case. Meed's suretyship ensures nothing for the future; it is rather a bribe to Peace and the king to drop the case.

Legally there was nothing against the king accepting this lucrative advice, and in practice the English court of King's Council did so. The case of the parson of Langay is one example; the case of the Earl of Devonshire is another. He has already been mentioned to indicate the effectiveness of the *subpoena*, which forced him to appear before the council in 1391 with his murderous retainer Robert Yeo. He need not have worried. When he was before the Council he actually admitted maintaining Yeo at law, and at first it seemed as though justice would be done — but blood is thicker than water:

> Whereupon it was adjudged by our lord the king and his said Council that the said earl of Devonshire should be committed to prison, there to remain until he had paid ... fine and ransom. ... Immediately thereafter all the aforesaid lords, spiritual as well as temporal, prayed our lord the king to do grace to the said earl ... having regard for the fact that he was of royal blood ... and that it was the first time any such complaint had been made to our lord the king against the said earl ... Our lord the king at the aforesaid request extended to the earl grace and pardon in his behalf, in condition that he should aid and sustain according to his power the laws of our said lord the king.[29]

Eventually the murderer, Robert Yeo, was also pardoned. What is perhaps even worse is that during the whole of this process the Earl never ceased to attend the ordinary meetings of the Council. In Langland's England Meed was indeed one of the Councillors of the King.

49

The *Visio* King however ignores those legal methods which direct him to have mercy on Wrong. He realises that this mercy only implies mercilessness to the poor and peaceable men whom Wrong oppresses. He insists on justice, appealing not to his law of his Council for authority, but to the equity which Conscience and Reason represent:

> 'Nay, by Crist' quod þe kyng, 'for Consiences sake
> Wrong goth nat so away ar y wete more.
> Lope he so lihtliche, lawen he wolde
> And efte the baldore be to bete myn hewes.
> Bute Resoun haue reuth on hym he shal reste in my stokkes'
>
> C.IV.99-103

He is right not to trust the rest of his Council; they immediately appeal for mercy for Wrong as the Council in 1391 had appealed for mercy for the Earl of Devonshire!

> Summe men radden Resoun tho to haue reuthe vppon þat shrewe
> And for to consayle þe kynge on Conscience thei lokede
>
> C.IV.105-6

However, like the ideal absolute monarch, the king listens to the voice of natural reason speaking within his own soul and rejecting false law and false counsel:

> 'And,' quod Resoun 'by þe rode, y shal no reuthe haue,
> Whiles Mede hath the maistrie þer motyng is at barres . . .
> Shulde neuere wrong in this worlde þat y wyte myhte
> Be vnpunisched in my power for perel of my soule.'
>
> C.IV.131-2, 136-7

Both Meed and Wrong are accordingly imprisoned, and, it must be said, the whole Council finally approves this decision.

3. The political implications of the king's triumph

It was perhaps after he had described the *Visio* king's success in restoring justice to his kingdom that Langland went back to his Prologue and revised it in the C-text to provide a more absolutist introduction to his discussion of kingship. The king in the final version of the Coronation Scene is guided by 'kynde wit' (*naturalis ratione*) and Conscience, and in now way by the 'commune' of England, The king in *Passus* IV is guided by Reason and Conscience, and in no way by the other Councillors or even his poor commoner, Peace. The king in the final version of the Coronation Scene shares his power to make law with none, and is indeed responsible for imposing justice or

50

'lewte' rather than for upholding the law. The king in *Passus* IV is disillusioned with a law that can be obscured by lawyers and obstructed by Meed; he too cares more for 'leutee':

> And lourede vppon men of lawe and lyhtlych sayde . . .
> 'Mede and men of ȝoure craft muche treuthe letteth . . .
> Y wol haue leutee for my lawe and late be al ȝoure iangling.'
>
> C.IV.168, 170, 174

Like the cat in the rat fable he needs to be unbelled so as to deal with vermin.

But suppose the *Visio* king were to turn into the tyrant cat? Absolutism is a dangerous form of government, and English history was moving against it. The Commons in Parliament were suspicious of the growing powers of the Council, which was expected to serve the king's interests and develop his absolutist powers, in contradiction to his subjects' Common Law rights. After all, it was traditionally the Commons which 'impeached' evil councillors, not the councillors themselves. The Articles of Deposition drawn up against Richard II accused him of using his Council to bypass both Common Law and Parliament.[30]

Reason in *Passus* IV seems to be aware of this kind of suspicion, and he only agrees to be the king's Chancellor on the condition that the king should continue to obey him. The Commons in Parliament generally wanted to restrain the king by law; Langland only wants him to be restrained by Reason, like the absolutist Wycliffe:

> Although . . . the king may dispense with the execution of the law in a particular case, as if superior to his own law, he may never do so unless reason so requires.[31]

Reason is more specific than Wycliffe; he warns the king against situations in which he might use his prerogative to serve self-interest rather than equity:

> 'Y assente' sayde Resoun 'by so ȝowsulue yhere
> *Audiatis alteram partem* amonges aldremen and comeneres,
> And þat vnsittynge suffraunce ne sele ȝoure priue lettres
> Ne no *supersedeas* sende but y assente,' quod Resoun.
>
> C.IV.187-90

In the first place the king must not imitate Common Law courts in favouring rich suitors, like aldermen, over poor commoners, but in accordance with the Roman law maxim, must 'hear the other party'.[32] Indeed the only justification for prerogative courts that the Commons and Parliament recognised, was that they did sometimes provide equity when the Common Law would not, particularly when one party is so great and rich, & the other so poor, that he could not otherwise recover his right.[33]

In the second place the king must not use 'priue lettres' (presumably those sealed by his official Privy Seal) to protect his friends, or those who could pay, from the rigour of the law. Langland probably added this complaint against 'vnsittynge suffraunce', together with the similar complaint which Conscience made in C.III. 207, during the early years of Richard II's reign (both passages only appear in the C-text). If so, it would have had a definite relevance, though once again it would have been a boy-king's tolerance or 'suffraunce', rather than an adult king's responsibility, that was attacked. For example in the first year of his reign there were issued over seventy writs of *supersedeas*, more than double the number issued in the whole of the last decade of Edward III's reign. Thereafter they came thick and fast. These would have released prisoners, prevented declarations of outlawry, and suspended legal hearings of all kinds -- generally for no better reason than the fee paid by a suitor.[34] Similarly in 1377 the king was asked to restrain the issue of 'priue lettres':

> because the law of the land and the Common Right has been often delayed by letters issued . . . under the Privy Seal of the king and the secret Signet, to the great grievance of the people[35]

The abuse continued, and in later years Richard even used his Privy Seal to suspend statutes, as one chronicler complained:

> Of what use are statutes made in Parliament? They have no effect. The King and his privy council habitually alter and efface what had previously been established in Parliament.[36]

Though this refers to a period after the time that Langland had finished revising his poem, it indicates that Reason's suspicions of how the prerogative power could be abused were quite justified.

On the other hand Langland suggests that so long as an absolutist king did restrain his prerogative by Reason, he would win the love of his subjects. Reason promises the *Visio* king this, in words which are the final rejoinder to Meed's offer to buy him both glory and friends:

> 'And y dar lege my lyf þat loue wol lene þe seluer,
> To wage thyn and helpe wynne þat thow wilnest aftur,
> More than alle thy marchauntes or thy mytrede bysshopes
> Or Lumbardus of Lukes þat leuen by lone as Iewes.'
>
> C.IV.191-4

Reason is here echoing the suspicions of many fourteenth-century Parliaments. They recognised that the king often needed capital sums over and above the money he received from traditional sources or the occasional grants of taxes. But they did not like him borrowing from foreigners, who expected protection and privileges in return. Between 1377 and 1389 Richard II's total 'genuine' borrowing amounted to some £156,000, and as much as £44,682 of this was borrowed from London merchants, £48,294 from alien merchants, and £10,005 from bishops. His largest single creditors were two Lombards, Matthew Cheyne and Antony Bache, who lent him £27,561 between them. One need only look at the Parliament Records for 1376 to see with what suspicion the Lombards were regarded; they were even accused of harbouring 'Jews . . . Saracens, and Privy Spies'.[37]

As an alternative to this dangerous dependence on self-interested (and mostly interest-charging) men, Reason offers the king loans made out of love. This was not as far-fetched as it sounds. In 1379 for example, during an invasion scare:

> all the lords there [in Parliament] voluntarily offered various great sums of money to our lord the king for the defence of the realm.[38]

However before they obtained this promise the ruling Council had to promise in its turn to clean up its own administration. Reason also makes the community's generosity depend on the king acting with justice and self-restraint. He is in fact voicing the principle that the subject expects justice in return for supporting the king, a principle which Conscience will express to the tyrant-king in *Passus* XXI, and which he has already explained to the *Visio* king in *Passus* III:

> 'As a kyng to clayme the comune at his wille
> To folowe and to fynde hym and fecche at hem his consayl . . .
> So comune claymeth of a kyng thre kyne thynges,
> Lawe, loue and lewete, and hym lord antecedent,
> Bothe heued and here kyng, haldyng with no partey3e'
>
> C.III.374-5, 377-381

This is the 'relacoun rect' which embodies Langland's political ideal: a kingdom where loving subjects serve an impartial king who uses his power to enforce justice.

Passus IV has in fact been the culmination not only of the 'Vision of Lady Meed and the King' but of the whole discussion of kingship in the *Visio*. The king has chosen to fulfil the promise of his coronation. His chosen councillors are Reason and Conscience, the spokesmen of God in his soul. He has asserted his absolute power in obedience to their guidance, and has driven both Meed and Wrong from his court. Will awakes from his vision with Reason's promise of an ideal social harmony ringing in his ears.

But the *Visio* king is not, finally, Richard II. Will awakens to a kingdom which is still divided by ambitious retinues and disrupted by crime. It is moreover threatened by another social problem which no king, however powerful or just, could solve single-handed: the problem of the Waster. When the king has failed, or when the king could not have succeeded, it is the subjects themselves who must take on some responsibility for social harmony and justice. But to do this they need leaders who will teach them their part in 'relacoun rect'. From now on Langland will describe leaders who are also subjects, whom I will call the 'subject-kings'.

Nor could the *Visio* king, even at the end of *Passus* IV, be wholly Langland's ideal of kingship. For all kings should imitate God, and although God is of course nothing if not absolute, Langland believed that He was also nothing if not merciful. We know the *Visio* king is right when he refuses to 'haue reuthe' on Wrong. But when standing before Christ all mankind is in the position of Wrong. Is Christ to enforce justice as the *Visio* king did, and condemn all mankind to Hell without the possibility of 'maynprise' or pardon? Why should He feel anything but anger against sin, and a desire to punish it as it deserves? Christ can only learn mercy, in Langland's analysis, if He too becomes a 'subject-king' not separated from His subjects by superior wisdom or power, but sharing their weakness and their sorrows.

The leaders I shall be discussing in the last chapter of this study are taken from *Passus* which cannot sustain the wholesale political analysis I have given to the Prologue and *Passus* II-IV. But they are also taken from dramatic visions, where Langland shows men in action, and where obedience to the law is still essential — though the laws themselves now often have a religious dimension. Obedience is however no longer enforced from above; it is taught from below, by the example of the 'subject-kings': Piers Plowman, Christ, and Conscience. They show us the way, but they do not force us to follow it, and in leaving us our freedom they leave us the glory of achievement. Now Langland writes not as an absolutist, but as a fervent and mystical democrat.

IV

THE SUBJECT-KINGS

With *Passus* IV we virtually come to the end of Langland's discussion of earthly kingship. He has established his ideal of an absolute monarch whose wisdom is greater than his people's, and whose power is above their laws. The *Visio* king, like Aquinas' ideal monarch,

> has assumed the duty of being to his kingdom what the soul is to the body and what God is to the universe ... appointed to administer justice throughout his realm in the name of God.[1]

The rest of his analysis of government centres not on the king of England, typified and idealised as the *Visio* king, but on Christ, the Divine model for all kings. However, neither Christ, nor His human agents, Piers Plowman and Conscience, act like absolute monarchs with regard to the law. They could be considered as 'limited monarchs', for they obey the same laws as do their subjects. But with the exception of the triumphant Christ, none of them assume any royal authority at all. Instead they demonstrate the subject's part in maintaining the 'relacoun rect' between a just king and his obedient people, described by Conscience in *Passus* III:

> 'Ac relacoun rect is a ryhtful custume,
> As a kyng to clayme the comune at his wille
> To folwe and to fynde hym and fecche at hem his consayl
> That here loue to his lawe thorw al þe lond acorde.
>
> C.III.373-6

The first of these 'subject-kings' is Piers the Ploughman. On his half-acre strip, described in *Passus* VIII, as in the *Visio* kingdom described in *Passus* II-IV, law by itself fails to establish justice. But unlike the *Visio* king Piers is not in a position to impose his own idea of justice on his recalcitrant employees, even if he wanted to. It is the community, rather than the king or his representatives, who share the responsibility for social justice and harmony here. And as the passage is allegorised as a pilgrimage to Truth, it also suggests that men's voluntary obedience to the laws of the land is part of their wider obedience to the laws of God. This leads one to ask what kind of laws Christ the king of kings tries to impose in the poem, and how He uses His (obviously absolute) authority.[2] Langland answers this question through the legal allegories of the Atonement which occur in *Passus* XVIII-XX. Once again we are shown a ruler who obeys the law as if He were His humblest subject. By so doing He releases mankind from the punishment they had incurred for failing to obey the law in Eden.

Man is then left, in the final Vision (*Passus* XXI-XXII) to obey only Conscience's law of *redde quod debes*, but Conscience has even less authority over his subjects than Piers had over his employees. He can be successful only if men crown him king in their own souls, and obey his advice as if he had absolute power. In spite of his earlier suggestions for political reform, Langland ends the poem with a plea for moral reform. He began by demonstrating the value of absolutism; he ends by demonstrating the responsibility of the 'commune'. Social harmony is only one aspect of the Universal Harmony; the political well-being of a kingdom is only the result of the moral well-being of both king and people.

1. Piers the Ploughman and the Waster

The threat to social justice and harmony which preoccupied Langland in *Passus* III and IV was Lady Meed. She and her followers were counteracted by the absolute power of a wise king. During the conflict Conscience explained how each subject could counteract Meed (in her widest sense) for himself, by working for 'mercede' instead.[3] 'Mercede', a word derived from *merces*, the Latin for reward, is a much clearer embodiment of the 'Mede . . . mesurable' described in the B-text (III. 231-258). It represents the just wage paid for work completed to the subject who lives according to reason and truth:

> 'And gylours gyuen byfore and goode men at þe ende
> When þe dede is ydo and þe day endit;
> And þat is no mede but a mercede, a manere dewe dette, . . .
> And ther is resoun as a reue rewardynge treuthe
> That bothe the lord and the laborer be leely yserued.'
>
> C.III.302-4, 308-9

We notice two important characteristics of *mercede*: it is paid in acknowledgement of a debt, and it represents a loyal and sympathetic contract between employer and servant. Both are characteristics of the 'relacoun rect' which should, as Conscience goes on to say, subsist between king and subject, or between God and the believer, as between employer and servant:

> 'Relacoun rect,' quod Consience, 'is a recorde of treuthe, . . .
> As a leel laborer byleueth þat his maister
> In his pay and in his pite and in his puyr treuthe
> To pay hym yf he parforme and haue pite yf he faileth
> And take hym for his trauaile al þat treuthe wolde.'

C.III.343, 347-350

After *Passus* IV the scene changes from the haunts of noble-women and kings to the fields and cottages where the 'comune' live. In *Passus* V-VIII (B.V-VI) Langland describes the community's disobedience to the laws of God and the Church, their penitence, and their search for Truth, that is, for a kind of life which will be both a penance for sin and a protection against it. At this point Piers Plowman appears for the first time in the poem and offers to show them his kind of life, which he allegorises not as a journey, but as service to a master who gives both the just 'mercede', and the sympathetic loyalty characteristic of 'relacoun rect':

> 'He is þe presteste payere þat eny pore man knoweth; . . .
> He is as louh as a lombe and leel of his tonge'

C.VII.195-7

Those sinners who share Piers' life on his half-acre will find, in the next *Passus*, that they have completed a pilgrimage to Truth and earned his pardon.

> Alle libbyng laborers þat lyuen with here handes
> Lellyche and lauhfollyche, oure lord Treuthe hem graunteth
> Pardon perpetuel, riht as Peres the plouhman.

C.IX.58-60

It seems that a good Christian must first be a good subject. Piers' labourers will fulfil their religious duty to God in the course of ful-filling their social duty to earn their bread honestly, and in loyalty to Piers and their fellow-subjects.

Langland's view of social duty in all these passages coincides closely with that of the fourteenth-century legislators, who for the first time were having to enforce the loyalty and honest work supposedly implicit in the ancient feudal system. By the beginning of the century that system was already breaking down on the manor. Many serfs were paying for their land in rent rather than in customary services, and an increasing number ran away to the towns. Lords were compelled to hire more and more labourers to work their demesnes. The situation was suddenly brought to a crisis by the Black Death, which wiped out about a third of the population in 1348-9. The 'free labourers' and serfs who remained began in much greater numbers to ignore their contracts with their employers or their feudal obligations to lords, and to wander throughout England seeking the highest wage for their services. A diminished population enjoying higher wages also exacerbated 'the problem of the pauper — the man who cannot or will not maintain himself by his work'.[4]

For the first time laws were needed to make every labourer find employment under fair terms, and to hold to those terms faithfully. The Statutes of Labourers passed between 1349 and the end of the century ordered all able-bodied men to find some means of support, and forbad any to give alms to those who might work if they chose. They regulated the wages that could be offered or accepted for particular jobs (outlawing extra 'perks' and inducements), and penalised labourers who left their employers before the term of service — usually a year — had expired.[5]

Piers Plowman meets the same problem that confronted Langland's governors, and tries to impose the same standards. He is not however working from a distance, as they were, but is himself both employer and labourer, and it is only at first that he can obey the statutes, and enforce 'mercede' or 'relacoun rect'. He intends to hire labourers for a full year, from harvest to harvest,[6] and to pay only those who work honestly:

> Now is Perkyn and þis pilgrimes to þe plouh faren;
> To erien this half-aker holpen hym monye.
> Dikares and deluares digged vp þe balkes;
> Therwith was Perkyn apayed and payed wel hem here huyre. . . .
> At hey prime Peres leet þe plouh stande
> And ouersey hem hymsulue; ho-so beste wrouhte
> He sholde be huyred þeraftur when heruost tyme come.'
>
> C.VIII.112-5, 119-121

When some labourers tire of work he refuses to pay them (122-7), and when these pretend to be disabled and 'fayned hem blynde' (128), he conforms to the Statute 23 Edward III chapter 7 in refusing them 'Pity or Alms . . . so that thereby they may be compelled to labour for their necessary Living':

> 'Ʒe been wastours, y woet el, and waste and deuouren
> What lele land-tilynge men leely byswynken.
> Ac Treuthe shal teche Ʒow his teme to dryue

Or ȝe shal ete barly breed and of þe broke drynke,
But yf he be blynde or broke-legged or bolted with yren'

C.VIII.139-143

We know that Piers is right to try to conform to the fourteenth-century labour laws, for this is not the first time in the poem that they have formed Langland's conceptualisation of the life of a good subject. In *Passus* V Reason (often thought of as the basis for all just laws) had condemned Will himself for not obeying them:

'Can thow seruen,' he sayde, 'or syngen in a churche,
Or koke for my cokeres or to þe cart piche,
Mowen or mywen or make bond to sheues . . .'

C.V.12-4

It is true that long before the Black Death had exacerbated the labour problem local custom, and even special by-laws known as the 'Statuti Autumpni', had obliged all able-bodied men and women in a village to help with the harvest.[7] But Reason's embarrassing questions reveal a greater affinity with the government's new legislation than with these old feudal obligations. For one thing Will is not a countryman, and yet Reason urges him to find harvest employment, just as a statute of 1388 was to urge servants and apprentices of whose work

a Man hath no great Need in harvest Time . . . [to] serve in Harvest, to cut gather and bring in the Corn.[8]

For another thing, Reason is conforming to the terms of the very first Statute of Labour when he asks Will, somewhat disingenuously, whether he has other means of support besides his labour:

'Thenne hastow londes to lyue by,' quod Resoun, 'or lynage ryche
That fynde the thy fode?'

C.V.26-7

Will's confession that he does indeed depend on alms for his subsistence proves his conscious disobedience of the statute, which required

every Man and Woman . . . able in body and . . . not . . . having of his own whereof he may live . . . to serve him which so shall him require.[9]

Thus in *Passus* V as in *Passus* VIII Langland expresses the opinion that a fundamental — almost a Divine — law backs those laws which impose honest and faithful work on the subject. Only Will's moral 'perfection' justifies him earning his bread in alms, by the labour of the spirit:

'Preyeres of a parfit man and penaunce discret
Is the leuest labour þat our lord pleseth.'

C.V.84-5

Since the prayers of the 'cripples' on Piers' half-acre were hardly so perfect (C.VIII.131-7) we are not surprised that they fail to justify their idleness, and indeed soon turn into threats:

Thenne gan Wastor to wrath hym and wolde haue yfouhte . . .
A Bretener cam braggyng, a bostede Peres also:
'Wolle thow, nulle thow,' quod he, 'we wol haue oure wille,
And thy flour and thy flesch feche whenne vs liketh . . .'

C.VIII.149, 152-4

According to a Commons petition of 1376, this is what 'faitours' who refused to work generally did:

Many of them become 'staff-strikers' and lead an idle life, commonly robbing poor people in simple villages.[10]

The Commons asked that such vagrants be put in the stocks or the nearest gaol. As a matter of fact the stocks had been a penalty for offenders against the Statutes of Labourers since 1350, and were widely used by the J.P.s who enforced the Statutes after 1361.[11] Piers accordingly turns for help to his own local knight, presumably appealing to him in his capacity of a J.P., rather than as a private landowner (who would enforce discipline on his own manor by means of a fine):

Peres the plouhman tho pleynede hym to þe knyhte
To kepe hym and his catel as couenant was bitwene hem: . . .
Courteisliche the knyhte thenne, as his kynde wolde,
Warnede Wastour and wissede hym betere:
'Or y shal bete the by the lawe and brynge þe in stokkes.'

C.VIII.156-7, 161-3

The knight does not however bring out the stocks, and Waster ignores his threat. As so often in the *Visio* kingdom the law somehow fails at the crucial moment to enforce justice. It is as if Langland shares the desires and aims of the fourteenth-century legislators, but not their 'delusion that in matters social and economic one can accomplish everything by laws and regulations'.[12]

And here we come to the telling difference between government by the *Visio* king, and government by Piers the subject. The king had used his absolute power to enforce justice when law had failed. But although the knight, the king's representative, has the power to imprison Waster, he does not use it, and Piers has to call in Hunger instead. This is the natural force which the laws were trying to avert, and which Piers, as a member of the community, feels as keenly as his fellow-subjects. It is a weapon which cannot be used by the king or the judges in their well-fed comfort, and it works for a time (C.VIII.167-324). But in an allegorical nicety Hunger is so effective at making men work and produce food, that he drives himself away. The Wasters then either return to begging, or break their contract with Piers and wander in search of higher wages:

> And tho wolde Wastor nat worche bote wandren aboute,
> Ne no beggare eten bred þat benes ynne were,
> Laborers þat han no lond to lyue on but here handes
> Deynede noȝt to dyne a-day of nyhte-olde wortes;
> May no peny-ale hem pay ne no pece of bacoun
> But hit be fresh flesch or fisch, yfried or ybake, . . .
> And but yf he be heyliche yhuyred elles wol he chydde . . .
> And thenne a corseth þe kyng and alle þe kynges iustices,
> Suche lawes to lerne, laboreres to greue.
>
> C.VIII.325-340 *passim*.

Here Langland specifically refers to the 'lawes' (340) which try to make labourers accept the old — and proper — conditions. Waster defies them not only by wandering,[13] but by demanding a 'courtesie' in lieu of higher wages, like the Lincolnshire ploughman described as typical by Miss Putman:

> he refuses to serve except by the day and unless he has fresh meat instead of salt, and finally leaves the town because no-one dares engage him on these terms.[14]

One can however see from this case that the labour laws were not as ineffective as Langland implies. In real life the Justices of the Peace did use the laws to enforce the principles which Conscience defined as 'mercede' and 'relacoun rect': keeping wages fair and strengthening contracts, making 'Waster' work and keeping Hunger at bay. Why then does *Passus* VIII end more with the triumph than the defeat of Waster, and with a warning that Hunger will return?

The answer must be that Langland was trying to demonstrate something different from the successfulness of a just force demonstrated at the end of *Passus* IV. Piers has no power over his labourers; that is the essence of his relationship with them, and it means that they are free to disobey in a way that Meed and Wrong, who are brought before the king's prerogative court, were not. This would not be the case if the half-acre were a traditional manor, and the labourers were the knight's bondsmen. Instead Langland describes a peasant (who is a ploughman inasmuch as all peasants must plough, though he may of course be a professional ploughman), cultivating that typical unit of peasant agriculture, the half-acre strip of land.[15] He and not the knight organises the estates and employs the labour. Far from being traditional, this social model describes one of the most recent developments in rural life:

61

The closing 150 years of the Middle Ages were marked by a profound transformation in agriculture. The capitalist or quasi-capitalist economy in demesne or monastic granges [i.e. where the landowner farmed the land himself through labourers and bondsmen] was invaded and conquered by peasant units.[16]

The lords were renting their demesnes to peasants like the two bondsmen in Forncett, Norfolk, who leased the entire arable land of the demesne (166½ acres) while still paying the lord commutation for the labour services they were now performing on their own behalf.[17] Such peasants, like Piers, would preside in a small community of equals, for they would have none of the manorial control over their employees that a lord had over his bondsmen. For this reason life on Langland's half-acre, besides corresponding more closely to contemporary developments than the traditional estates model, also provides a closer analogy with the life of the Christian. It shows the connection between the free subject, who chooses whether or not he will labour honestly for himself and for the community as a whole, and the free Christian, who chooses whether or not to sin.

Furthermore Piers, who shares his labourers' work and their hunger, feels more like a brother towards them than like a lord or a king. Truth may have taught him the principle of just deserts, but he prefers to remember his own side in the 'relacoun rect' and shrinks from starving the Wasters into submission to his will:

> Treuthe tauhte me ones to louye hem vchone
> And to helpe hem of alle thynges ay as hem nedeth.

C.VIII.218-9

Hunger's advice that Piers should provide only 'houndes bred and hors breed' (225) for the Waster is much more charitable than the strict terms of the Statute of 1349, which forbad all such alms. It is not only in the B-text then that Piers puts charity before justice; in both texts only Hunger's authoritative harangue prevents him from breaking the Statute even more.[18]

It is in fact Piers' charitableness, and not his sternness to Wasters, which will be remembered at the end of the poem, and contrasted with the cruelty of the official leaders of the Church:

> 'Rihte so Peres the plouhman payneth hym to tulie
> As wel for a wastour or for a wenche of the stuyves
> As for hymsulue and his seruauntes, saue he is furste yserued.'

C.XXI.434-6

This makes the analogy between life on the half-acre and the life of a Christian even closer, for Piers' charity is of course modelled on Christ's. The Church, like the pilgrims on the half-acre, is led by one who shared men's sorrows and forgives their shortcomings. The government of Christ is necessarily more merciful than the government of the *Visio* king.

Unfortunately for the pilgrims, Truth is not as charitable as Piers. In the next *Passus* (C.IX; B.VII) he denies pardon to those who have not laboured honestly in society. Although some poor unfortunates and some genuine men of religion are excused their physical responsibilities to their fellow-subjects, he condemns absolutely the 'religious wasters' (the 'lollares' of C.IX.140-174, 188-254) who labour neither with their hands nor in their prayers. His pardon embodies the justice, not the mercy of God; in Conscience's terms, it leans more towards 'mercede' than 'relacoun rect':

> 'Peter!' quod the prest tho, 'y kan no pardoun fynde,
> Bote "Dowel and haue wel and god shal haue thy soule . . .
> Bote he þat euele lyueth euele shal ende".'
>
> C.IX.290-1, 3

It would seem that if God governs through this Truth mankind will be treated as justly as the *Visio* king treated Wrong.

The tension between the justice of Truth and the mercy of Piers is expressed best in the B-text, where Piers tears Truth's pardon. In the C-text this does not happen, so that at this stage in the poem God's Truth seems to dominate. In a way this makes a satisfying contrast between the *Visio* kingdom, fighting to control the power of Meed, Wrong and Waster, and the Kingdom of Heaven, where such evils will be excluded. But for this very reason it is an unsatisfactory conclusion, for has not the whole experience of the *Visio* been that men are corrupt and cannot consistently 'Dowel'? They need a ruler like Piers, who will encourage the good in them by example or by threats, and not one who will exile them from his kingdom. It is in fact Piers, and not the *Visio* king or Truth, who will prove to be most closely modelled on Christ the King of Heaven, through whose life God's Truth and His mercy are reconciled.

2. Christ as subject and king

The problem of how God's justice can be reconciled with His mercy is answered by Christians in the 'doctrine of the Atonement'. Following St Paul,[19] theologians argued that Christ fulfilled in His own person the demands of God's justice by dying on the cross for man's Original Sin. This released Adam's descendants from Hell, and thereafter men had the chance of being judged, and even pardoned, their failures to obey Christ's New Law of love. There is nothing unusual in Langland centering his poem on Christ's Atonement. What are original are the parallels he finds for it in England law, which enable it to be related to the theme of government running through the whole poem.

Christ's life is discussed in the section of the poem known as *Dobet* (C.XVIII-XX), and here the Atonement is introduced first as a *bail* which Christ must purchase to release mankind from prison (C.XVIII.278-286). He acts in this as a subject of God the Father, compelled to abide by the terms of the Old Law. In the next *Passus* the Atonement is spoken of as a *seal* on the Charter of the New Law which Christ, now a king, can give to His subjects (C.XIX.1-15). In *Passus* XX Christ again acts as a subject, a knight, who fights a *duel* in order to prove His right to possess mankind (C.XX.1-113, 271-449). With the winning of the duel Christ recovers His rights as king, and *pardons* mankind their sin — being careful however to buy this pardon as if He were His own subject (C.XX.421-431). All four of these images involve a *quid pro quo* which Christ, as subject to the Old Law, pays before He can give mankind the benefits of the New Law. His life as a subject does not only provide an example for His brother-men, as Pier's life on the half-acre did, but also buys for mankind their release from Hell. He acts throughout as if He were a 'subject king', limited by a law not of His own making, and which is allegorised as the English law which Langland's own readers must also obey. The dual nature of Christ as man and God is in fact related to the dual role of all kings to be both below and above the law.

(a) Bail: C.XVIII.278-286 (B.XVI.261-269)

It will be remembered that in *Passus* IV Lady Meed offered the *Visio* king an alternative to punishing Wrong. She offered to stand as 'borw' or 'mainpernour' for him: in other words, she would pledge or 'wage' a large security of money which she would lose to the king if Wrong offended again (C.IV.83-98; see above pp.48-49). The king however refused to bail or 'mainprise' Wrong in this way, because he knew that Meed would not mind losing money so long as Wrong could go on acting with the same brutal licence.

In *Passus* XVIII we learn that all Adam's descendants, (allegorised as the fruit from the Tree of True Love) have been imprisoned by the devil. Langland then uses the same legal terms that he used in *Passus* IV, but it is now mankind, not Wrong, who needs to be bailed. By recalling the earlier situation in his re-use of technical language, Langland is putting the political question: will the king of Heaven govern with less justice than the earthly *Visio* king if He allows man to be mainprised?

Justice is maintained because different kinds of security are offered in the two cases. Meed (in a recent use of the word 'mainprise') offered only money as security for Wrong's future good conduct if left at large. Abraham however needs a surety ('borw') prepared to purchase the original writ of mainprise. This only released a man from prison until his trial, and theoretically committed the bailor to stand 'body for body' ('corpus pro corpore') in place of the bailee if he absconded before then.[20] Christ will offer as security ('wed for vs wagen') His own body and life, and the devils may retain this life in return for releasing their far less valuable prisoners:

> 'may no wed vs quyte
> Ne noen bern ben oure borw ne bryngen vs out of þat daunger
> Fro þe poukes pondefold no maynprise may vs feche
> Til he come þat y carpe of, Crist is his name,
> That shal delyuere vs som day out of þe deueles power
> And bettere wed for vs wagen then we ben alle worthy,
> And þat is lyf for lyf;'

C.XVIII.279-285

Abraham's bail imagery emphasises the legal forces which prevent mankind from freeing themselves, and also prevent Christ from simply rescuing them from prison. The bail imagery also implies that man is now pledged to stand trial at the Last Judgement, a possibility which was not open to Adam's descendents before the Crucifixion. Christ's readiness to pay the bail, as subject to the law of justice, will recover for Him His right to judge mankind as their king. It is then that He will act as justly as the *Visio* king did towards Wrong:

> And demen hem at domesday, bothe quyke and dede,
> The gode to godhede and to grete ioye
> And wikked to wonye in wo withouten ende.

C.XXI.196-8

(b) Charter: C.XIX.1-15 (B.XVII.1-15)

If Abraham was searching for a loving brother-subject to bail mankind, Moses, who follows him in *Passus* XIX, must find a king to seal his charter. And just as Christ's life was required to buy a mainprise for mankind, so it is now demanded as a seal for the 'letter patent' which gives a New Law of love to mankind. Before He can use His power as king to give new laws to His subjects, He must pay a *quid pro quo* to the devil who has been their lord since the Fall. Moses explains this to Will:

'y seke hym þat hath þe seel to kepe,
The which is Crist and cristendoem and croes þer-an yhanged.
Were hit þerwith aseled y woet wel þe sothe
That Luciferes lordschipe lowe sholde lygge.'
'Let se thy lettres,' quod y, 'we myhte þe lawe knowe.'
A pluhte forth a patente, a pece of an hard roche
Whereon was writen two wordes and on this wyse yglosed:
  Dilige deum et proximum. . . .
  In hiis duobus pependit tota lex.

C.XIX.7-13, 15

A 'letter patent' was a royal command or licence of 'public, general, permanent or recurrent application',[21] for which the seal must remain intact so as to authorise the document. It was accordingly attached by a tag to the bottom of the letter, and not used to seal it up, as on a 'letter close'. For this reason the Great Seal, which symbolised the kingdom as a whole (as 'key to the realm') had two faces, one for each side of the dangling piece of wax. The seal which Moses seeks also represents the whole kingdom of Christ, and will hang pendant from the letter to authorise the New Law of love it grants to all men. And of course, as Langland's choice of words implies, the king must pay the price, must hang from the cross in order that the seal may hang from the charter (8).

This allegory is not original to Langland. The various short literary pieces constructed as *Charters of Christ* in the fourteenth and fifteenth centuries also indicate that Christ sealed with His suffering a document granting eternal life to mankind:

  The selus þat it was seled wiþ
  They weron grauon on a stiþ
  Of gold ne seluer ne ben þei noȝt
  Of styl and yron þey weron wroȝt.[22]

However most of these 'charters' are set out as 'feoffments' or grants of land (the inheritance of Heaven). Christ's letter patent in *Piers Plowman* grants a new law instead. This not only stresses His royal power, but leaves man as big a part to play (in obeying the New Law) as the bail imagery of the previous *Passus* had done, so that once again the image looks forward to the Last Judgement. The king of Heaven suffered for His obedience to law, and has no intention of ruling without law.

(c) Duel: C.XX.1-113, 271-449 (B.XVIII.1-109, 263-406)

The legal allegorisation of the Atonement into which Langland poured most meaning and poetry is the duel of Christ with Lucifer on the Cross. Here he specifically relates Christ's readiness to be both subject and king to His double nature as man and God. In the next *Passus* Conscience will explain the theology behind this to Will (C.XXI. 26-198). 'Jesus' the man and knight became a king when He gave the Jews the New Law of love, but He only fully recovered His royal and Divine powers after He had become 'Christ' the Conqueror on the Cross. In *Passus* XX Jesus the man and subject wears the armour of Piers, which conceals Christ the God and king from Lucifer. Abraham (Faith) explains this to Will:

> 'this Iesus of his gentrice shal iouste in Pers armes,
> In his helm and in his haberion, *humana natura*,
> That Crist be nat ykowe for *consummatus deus*,
> In Pers plates the plouhman this prikiare shal ryde,
> For no dount shal hym dere as *in deitate patris*.'

C.XX. 21-5

So far Langland is using the allegory of a 'marvellous battle' between Life and Death found in essence in the Easter liturgy, and developed in medieval vernacular writings, of which Nicholas Bozon's early fourteenth-century version is probably the closest to Langland's. In this, Christ takes the arms of His bachelor Adam in order to tempt Belial into fighting Him. As soon as Belial fells Him and strips off His armour, He is revealed in His own arms 'entirely quartered with joy and with life', and He can defeat Belial and rescue His beloved from Hell.[23]

Langland does not ignore the element of trickery in Christ's disguise as a man. Mercy will call it a 'goed sleythe' (C.XX.165) suggesting thereby the chivalric concept of a *bonus dolus*, 'a fair trick to overcome an unfair one'.[24] But Christ justifies it carefully by insisting that Lucifer also tricked Adam by his disguise as a serpent (377-82). In any case it would be difficult to remove this deceitful aspect of Christ's action entirely, for not only in Bozon's poem, but in the *Gospel of Nicodemus* which first told the story of the Harrowing of Hell, Christ depends on His disguise to enter Hell and defeat Lucifer by force. Disguise and force are however hardly satisfying ways for Christ to overcome Lucifer, who does have rights over mankind since Adam's Original Sin. By setting the Harrowing of Hell within the medieval allegory of the Four Daughters of God, Langland indicates that his central concern is to reconcile God's mercy towards man with His justice towards the devil.[25] He does this by transforming the old idea of a straightforward battle or joust between Lucifer and a disguised Christ, into an allegory of a legal duel between two champions, Death and Life. A joust was a trial of strength in which the strongest man won; a duel was a legal ordeal: 'What triumphed was not brute force but truth.'[26] Langland's Christ, as subject to this

law, will prove on the body of Life that He has a right to rescue mankind and bind Lucifer.

There were three kinds of duel still being fought in fourteenth-
century England, though they were rare enough to be generally
accompanied by a good deal of publicity and make it probable that
Langland knew the rather sensational law involved.[27] Only one of
these, the 'civil duel of right', which decided the ownership of
property, involved champions (who would never of course appear in
a joust — though this is what Langland frequently calls his battle,
presumably because it alliterates with Jesus). At the beginning of
Passus XX Will dreams of Christ's entry into Jerusalem, and Abraham,
as we have seen, reappears to tell him that Christ is riding to a duel.
This will indeed decide the ownership of property, namely the 'fruit'
of patriarchs and prophets which the devil took when they fell from
the Tree of True Love (C.XVIII.111-130):

> 'Deth saith a wol fordo and adown brynge
> Alle þat lyueth or loketh, a londe or a watre
> Lyf saith þat a lyeth and hath leide his lyf to wedde,
> That for al þat Deth can do, withynne thre dayes to walke
> And feche fro þe fende Peres fruyt þe plouhman,
> And legge hit þere hym liketh and Lucifer bynde
> And forbete adown and brynge bale deth for euere.'

C.XX.28-34

In fact, when the allegorisation of this battle was first introduced in
Passus XVIII, *Spiritus Sanctus* told Mary that it would decide the
ownership of this property by 'iugement or armes' (XVIII.129), a
phrase evoking law rather than chivalry. Christ the just king will win
back His people in *Piers Plowman* by law, rather than by force or
fraud.

The 'civil duel of right' was a possible means of proof in cases
brought under the Writ of Right, which was the oldest and most
solemn proceeding to decide the seisin of land. The Writ was brought
by one who 'demanded' that he had inherited a better 'title' to the
'seisin' or feudal ownership of a particular property than the present
'tenant'. The demandant must prove that his ancestors had owned
the property before the present tenant's ancestors, and if all evidence
was lost, and the defendant refused a jury trial by Grand Assize, then
the issue was decided by a duel between champions chosen by the
parties. The champion who lost not only lost the cause for his
employer or 'principal', but some of his own civil rights as well. The
champion who won gained the disputed seisin for his principal and
his descendants for ever.[28]

We can assume that Christ is the demandant and claims that His
ancestor (who is of course Himself as 'sire . . . of heuene': 302)

owned mankind before the devil. We deduce this much from the answer Lucifer makes to His challenge in Hell: namely, that this property was granted to Lucifer by Christ's ancestor, and that he had been 'sesed' of it 'for a time ("seuene thousand wynter") sufficient to exclude any reasonable probability of a superior adverse claim ("and neuere was þer-aȝeyne")':[29]

> 'For hymsulue said hit, þat sire is of heuene,
> That Adam and Eue and all his issue
> Sholde deye with doel and here dwelle euere
> Yf they touched a tre or toek þerof an appul.
> Thus this lord of liht such a lawe made, . . .
> And sethen we haen ben sesed seuene thousand wynter,
> And neuere was þer-aȝeyne and now wolde bigynne,
> Thenne were he vnwrast of his word, þat witnesse is of treuthe.'
>
> C.XX. 302-6, 308-310

'Treuthe' or justice does indeed seem to be on Lucifer's side; a jury would have recognised both the length of his possession and, more importantly, the fact that he acquired it from the demandant's ancestor.[30] But Lucifer has not chosen trial by jury, but trial by battle, where the issue is decided not by argument but by the success of the champions.

The battle proceeds like a legal duel,[31] and it is not at first certain who will win. The champions, as was legally required, come in the arms of the principals whose 'rihte' is being judged before a court of law sitting in the lists:

> Thenne cam Pilatus with moche peple, *sedens pro tribunali*,
> To se how douhtyliche Deth sholde do, and demen þer beyre rihte.
>
> C.XX. 35-6

Jesus refuses the vinegar offered him on the Cross, just as a champion was supposed to refuse anything to eat or drink in the lists (52-3), and then He appears to die:

> The lord of lyf and of liht tho leyde his eyes togederes.
>
> C.XX. 60

The champion Death seems to have extinguished the 'lord of lyf', but dead bodies come alive to say that the duel is not lost, but truly begun:

> 'Lyf and Deth in this derkenesse here oen fordoth her oþer,
> Ac shal no wyht wyte witturlich ho shal haue þe maistry
> Ar a Soneday, aboute the sonne-rysynge'
>
> C.XX. 68-70

The last words, with the hidden pun on 'sonne-rysynge', intimate the true outcome of the duel, for the supremacy of Life is of course proved by the Resurrection.

69

Long before that, however, the Jews have their first indication that they have lost the duel. If Jesus is the human counterpart to Life the champion, then blind Longeus unwittingly becomes the human counterpart of Death when he is chosen as 'chaumpioun chiualer' (103) of the Jews. They need a human champion to 'iouste with Iesus' (85) and ensure that Death has overcome Him, but are afraid to touch Him themselves:

> For he was knyht and kynges sone, Kynde for3af þat tyme
> That hadde no boie hardynesse hym to touche in deynge.
>
> C.XX.79-80

Their fear shows of course that they suspect Jesus really is their king; the Ordinances of War collected in Richard II's reign threatened any who was 'so hardy as to touch the body of our lord [the King]' with a traitor's death.[32] And as soon as Longeus, miraculously cured by the blood he has shed, realises whom He has wounded, he offers his body and all his lands to his king as an 'escheat' or forfeit for this treason:

> 'Bothe my lond and my licame at 3oure likynge taketh hit,
> And haue mercy on me, ri3tfol Iesu!'
>
> C.XX.94-5

Faith takes Longeus' submission as a more ominous acknowledgement that he has lost the duel with Jesus by pronouncing, as the *Mirror of Justices* puts it, 'lorrible mot de cravent en noun de recreantise':

> 'The gre 3ut hath he [Jesus] geten for al his grete woundes,
> For 3oure chaumpioun chiualer, chief knyht of 3ow alle,
> 3elde hym recreaunt remyng, riht at Iesu wille'
>
> C.XX.102-4

A champion who 'cried recreant' not only lost his employer's cause, but his own right to be accounted a *liber et legalis homo* (a free and loyal man).[33] Faith gloatingly proves that this has happened to the Jews who identified themselves with their defeated champion. The medieval position of the Jews was to be that of serfs subject to arbitrary 'tribuyt and talage' (XXI.37) and unable to hold land:

> 'For be this derkenesse ydo, Deth worth yvenkused
> And 3e, lordeyns, haen lost, for Lyf shal haue maistrie,
> And 3oure franchise þat fre was yfallen is into thraldoem,
> And alle 3oure childerne cherles, cheue shal neuere,
> Ne haue lordschipe in londe ne no londe tulye'
>
> C.XX.105-9

Jews in England before their expulsion in 1290 were accounted the king's bondsmen, could be taxed or fined without reason, and were unable to hold land because they could not pronounce the Christian oath of vasselage.[34] Faith uses their unfortunate position as his final proof of the triumph of Life over Death.

The result of Life's victory can be seen the moment Christ enters the gates of Hell and claims back mankind, having proved on His body His more ancient right to them and their right to liberty:

> 'Lo me here,' quod oure lord, 'lyf and soule bothe,
> For alle synfole soules to saue oure bothe rihte.
> Myne they were and of me; y may þe bet hem clayme.'
> C.XX.370-2

Since Lucifer has been tricked into accepting a decisive duel with so invincible a champion, the devils must abide by his defeat and lose their seisin for ever:

> 'Bote leten hym lede forth which hym luste and leue which hym likede.
> C.XX.449

God's justice, which Lucifer distorted by tricking Adam and Eve to sin, has begun to be restored; 'Fals-doem' has begun to die. But this is not enough. Although Christ has regained His right to possess mankind, He still has to convict Lucifer of stealing mankind from Him. Accordingly the duel of Right which He fought as man's champion serves also as a duel of treason fought on His own behalf to restore His right to punish Lucifer.

Treason was the second of the three occasions on which duels were still fought in Langland's England, but it did not come under Common Law. Edward III had formalised this ancient martial procedure by placing it under his new Court of Chivalry, and in the later fourteenth century it was used several times by knights to answer a charge which challenged their very honour. The procedure was a more highly ritualised version of the duel of Common Law, though it was fought by the principals themselves, not their champions, and included some purely chivalric features.[35] Langland may have been present at two of the first duels to be fought under the Court of Chivalry, in 1350 and 1352, for duels always attracted large audiences.[36]

The devils in Hell are very much aware that Lucifer committed treason against Christ's 'loue and his leue' (314) — the allegiance and obedience due to a King. As Satan (rather treacherously) points out, Lucifer trespassed in Eden, disguised himself as a serpent, and told lies to deceive Adam and Eve (312-321):

> 'Thus with treson and tricherie thow troyledest hem bothe' C.XX.319

Gobelyne is afraid that this treason invalidates their title to mankind (323), and 'the fende' adds that this was not Lucifer's first treason,

71

and may well be punished like the first with the escheat of their estates to the King:

> 'For thy lesinges, Lucifer, we losten furst oure ioye, ...
> And now for a lattere lesing þat thow lowe til Eue,
> We haen ylost oure lordschipe a londe and in helle.'

C.XX.345, 348-9

That first treason in Heaven was even worse than the treason in Eden, for as Holy Church showed in *Passus* I, it was committed within the idealistic community of an Order of Knights chosen by the King Himself. It was accordingly punished (as the treason of a Knight of the Garter or Golden Fleece would be) by degredation as well as the escheat of estates:[37]

> 'He was an archangel of heuene, on of goddes knyghtes,
> He and oþer with hym helden nat with treuthe,
> Lepen out in lothly forme for his fals wille'

C.I.107-9

Now Lucifer must fear an even lower degradation.

When Christ comes in battle array to the gates of Hell the atmosphere is therefore already charged with treason. It may be that when Lucifer challenges Him in words which paraphrase Psalm 23 (Vulgate) as used in the *Gospel of Nicodemus*:

> 'What lord artow?' quod Lucifer. A voys aloude saide:
> 'The lord of myhte and of mayne, þat made alle thynges.

C.XX.360-1

that Langland was also thinking of the challenge to the appellant in a duel of treason:

> the appellaunt ... shall come to the gate of the listes in the Est in such maner as he wil fight ... and the conestable shall axe hym what man he is which is coomen armed to the gate of the listes, and what name he hath, and for what cause he is comyn.[38]

Christ wins this duel against Lucifer not as man's champion, but on His own behalf, by the power of His light and the force of His breath (364-369). At once He accuses Lucifer, repeating Satan's words, of treason 'aȝeyne my loue and my leue' (381, *cp*.314). Lucifer's treason had in fact robbed Christ the King of His subjects, removing them to Hell where He could neither judge nor protect them. He proves His recovery of kingship by pardoning mankind, and punishing the devils instead, for they were the causers of the Original Sin:

> 'Ac my rihtwysnesse and rihte shal regnen in helle'   C.XX.439

It is thus Lucifer and not mankind who becomes the true equivalent of Wrong in the *Visio*, and at this moment of triumph Christ recalls the words of Reason at his triumph over Meed and Wrong in the *Visio* parliament (C.IV.140-1):

> 'For holy writ wol þat y be wreke of hem þat wrouhte ille,
> As *nullum malum impunitum, et nullum bonum irremuneratum.*'
>
> C.XX.432-3

But Christ punishes Lucifer not only as His King, but also as a subject who has legally won the captivity of a traitor he has defeated in a fair duel, as the victor did in 1350:

> 'Ac for þe lesynge þat thow low, Lucifer, til Eue,
> Thow shal abyye bittere,' quod god, and bonde hym with chaynes.
>
> C.XX.445-6

The 'marvellous battle' in *Piers Plowman* does not merely prove that God is more powerful than Lucifer. Christ's life is the *quid pro quo* which proves first His right to free mankind, and then His right to bind Lucifer as a traitor.

(d) Pardon: C.XX.421-431 (B.XVIII.379-389)

From the moment that Christ recovers His subjects He recovers also His royal rights over them. But He has now experienced life as their brother and fellow-subject, and His impulse is to use His royal prerogative of pardon to remit all further punishment for them. A medieval king had this power to override the law, but could only do so under certain conditions, and if he also bound the pardoned subject to compensate those he had injured. Similarly Christ the King must observe the conditions, and must pay, as His own subject, to release mankind from all claims made by the devil. Once again Langland uses the dual role of a king to be both above and below the law as an allegory for the dual nature of Christ as both God and His own subject, man.

When He enters Hell Christ explains that it is his desire to pardon His blood-brothers, and that two of the traditional circumstances warranting a pardon obtain. In the first place the punishment has not killed the victim, and

> 'Hit is nat vsed on erthe to hangen eny felones
> Oftur then ones'
>
> C.XX.421-2

If the rope broke around the felon's neck (and sometimes it was frayed on purpose) he was pardoned, because in that his life is preserved by divine clemency, he may remain safe and sound in the kingdom of England.[39]

In the second place, if the king were present at a hanging he might prevent it, according to the ancient *Laws of Edward the Confessor*.[40] So also is Christ present in Hell to see man being punished, and so

> 'if lawe wol y loke on hem hit lith in my grace
> Where they deye or dey nat'

C.XX.428-9

Yet once again He can only grant as a king what He has paid for as a subject. A royal pardon only protected a murderer from prosecution by the crown; the victim's kin retained their ancient legal right to 'appeal' him by private suit. Consequently he had to 'make an accord' or settlement with them before he could enjoy the benefits of the pardon.[41] The Good Samaritan had used this fact in *Passus* XIX to emphasise that men must pay for their sins in penance before God will pardon them:

> 'Ther þat partye pursueth the apeel is so huge
> That may no kynge mercy graunte til bothe men acorde.'

C.XIX.283-4

Now Christ explains that He Himself has bought off the devil by giving His life in payment for man's Original Sin. This makes an 'accord' after which He can resume His royal prerogative of pardon:

> 'Be hit enythyng abouhte, the boldenesse of here synne,
> Y may do mercy of my rihtwysnesse and alle myn wordes trewe.'

C.XX.430-1

Since Christ has obeyed the law at His Crucifixion, He may dispense with it at the Last Judgement and pardon all penitent sinners.

Thus Christ's obedience to the Old Testament law enables God's justice to be reconciled with His mercy. Langland represents this in accordance with allegorical tradition, as the reconciliation of the Four Daughters of God. But he makes sure that Peace refers to the four legal terms under which that reconciliation was possible:

> 'For Iesus ioustede wel, ioy bigynneth dawe. . . .
> Loue, þat is my lemman, such lettres he me sente
> That Mercy, my sustur, and y mankynde shal saue,
> And þat god hath forgyue and graunted to alle mankynde,
> Mercy, my suster, and me to maynprisen hem alle;
> And þat Crist hath conuerted the kynde of rihtwisnesse
> Into pees and pyte, of his puyr grace.
> Loo, here þe patente!' quod Pees, '*in pace in idipsum* —
> And that this dede shal duyre — *dormiam et requiescam*.'

C.XX.184-192

Jesus' *joust* (or duel) has overcome Death. God has *pardoned* mankind. Love (Christ) has agreed to stand 'body for body' in place of man, so that Mercy and Peace may *mainprise* him. And Christ has sent a *patent* granting a New Law of love, and eternal peace in Heaven, to those He has forgiven. These concessions all depend on the *quid pro quo* which He has paid by His death. In this way Christ has set the standard of justice and mercy for all kings, as Aquinas had said:

> A king, then, should realise that he has assumed the duty of being to his kingdom ... what God is to the universe ... [and] be fired with zeal for justice ... and ... on the other hand ... grow in mildness and clemency, looking upon the persons subject to his government, as the members of his own body.[42]

Passus XX ends with an achieved 'relacoun rect' between the King of Heaven and His subjects and brothers. The theme of government in *Piers Plowman* culminates in this ideal, in which love, loyalty, and faithkeeping grow from the just foundation of a king who obeys the law and makes his subjects obey it as far as they can.

3. The reign of Conscience

Piers Plowman does not end with the triumph of Christ. The King of Heaven leaves the physical world and sends Grace to establish the new kingdom of *Unitas*. Once more the estates are marshalled, given duties, and commanded to hold together in fellowship (C.XXI.229-255). As in the earthly kingdom founded in the Prologue, the community is to provide for itself and to obey its leaders. Their king is Conscience, promoted from his position in the *Visio* as the king's Chief Justice, but without his wise counsellor, Reason.[43] He is assisted at first by Piers Plowman, who may now be identified with St Peter, the first Pope (C.XXI.182-190), and who enforces a law very similar to the law of just earning he enforced on his half-acre in *Passus* VIII. Grace gives them authority:

> And crouneth Consience kyng and maketh Craft ʒoure styward
> And aftur Craftes consail clotheth ʒow and fedeth.
> For y make Peres the plouhman my procuratour and my reue,
> And registrer to reseyuen *Redde quod debes.*'
>
> C.XXI.256-9

To 'render what you owe',[44] to pay both man and God the 'dewe dette' which was part of Conscience's definition of 'mercede' (C.III. 304), is to live both as a good subject and, through paying penance, as a good Christian.

Langland's name here for the Church, *Unitas*, suggests that he was referring to the 'Principle of Unity' which attracted many medieval writers on government, and suggested the ideal of a single Universal State (the Church) under a single leader (the Pope). As Gierke explains:

> Throughout the whole Middle Ages there reigned, almost without condition or qualification, the notion that the Oneness and Universality of the Church must manifest itself in a unity of law, constitution and supreme government, and also the notion that by rights the whole of Mankind belongs to the Ecclesiastical Society that is thus constituted.

However once again Langland seems to follow a more Wycliffite approach, for he suggests that this Universal Church 'should be conceived in a more inward . . . fashion'. Piers and Conscience are not really allegorisations of early Church leaders, as much as of forces within the different individuals who make up the Church as a whole. This was part of the same concept of Unity, for because of it:

> the self-same principles that appear in the structure of the World will appear . . . in the structure of its every part.[45]

Conscience then is put in the position of king to demonstrate that the Church on earth must be led from within the soul of every Christian. And since Christians are free to sin, Conscience has none of the absolute authority which the *Visio* king had over his Council. He is more akin to Piers in *Passus* VIII in trying to lead his fellowmen by example and counsel rather than by enforcing penalties. Therein lies his weakness, for when Unitas is attacked by Pride and Antichrist he cannot command the Christians to be faithful or even to take his advice. Langland accordingly allegorises his Church's increased disregard of Conscience, as the spread of treason within the kingdom of *Unitas*.

Langland had already used treason as an image for disobedience to God, most notably in Lucifer's case (see above, pp.71-2). But whereas his were individual crimes committed in a chivalric context, we are now shown the political failure of a whole society to keep 'leaute' or allegiance with its king. Because feudal society depended on such allegiances, treason was the most serious medieval crime. It had been formally defined by statute in 1352 in terms of offences against the king's person, family and image, and the more political offences involving 'open war against the king in his realm'.[46] Pride and Antichrist can be considered as traitors to Christ and Christendom when they come 'in manner of war' against the lawful king of *Unitas*:

76

> Auntecrist hadde thus sone hondredes at his baner
> And Pryde hit baer baldly aboute
>
> C.XXII.69-70

This bold display of the signs of war proves the treason:

> The display of banners .. was a recognised sign of open war and thereby
> constituted evidence that a traitor had levied war against the king in his
> realm . . .[47]

But Pride and Antichrist would scarcely admit they owed an
allegiance to Conscience; what is far more serious is that under their
banner come many former inhabitants of *Unitas*, Christians who are,
in the words of the statute, 'adherent to the king's enemies in his
realm'. These are committing treason to Christ as well as to
Conscience.

Langland continues to allegorise the moral corruption of the
Church as an unjust war which breaks the civilist 'Laws of War' as
well as the Common Law of England. Once Pride has prepared the
field by distorting the Christians' moral values (XXI. 336-355), Antichrist leads his army on a *dampnum* 'or destructive march:

> Auntecrist cam thenne, and al the crop of treuthe
> Turned hit tyd vp-so-down
>
> C.XXII.53-4

This strategy was only permitted in public war (such as Meed had
unjustly urged on the king in *Passus* III); it was forbidden in a
dispute with a leige-lord such as Conscience represents. The armies
then meet even before the heralds can officially begin the battle, and
what is worse, some of Conscience's army immediately break the
Ordinances of War by independently sounding the cry to retreat:[48]

> 'Alarme! alarme!' quod þat lord, 'vch lyf kepe his owene!'
> Thenne mette thise men, ar munstrals myhte pype
> And ar heroudes of armes hadden descreued lordes.
>
> C.XXII.92-4

During the pitched battle which follows there recur several con-
flicts from earlier in the poem, including the conflict between Covetousness and Conscience which had threatened the political stability
of the *Visio* kingdom. Covetousness is as it were a harsher embodiment of Meed, and is followed, as she was, by Simony. He enters the
King's Council and High Courts (which sat in Westminster Hall)
where he is more successful than Meed was in persuading the Justices
to accept an easy security in lieu of punishment for crimes:

> And cam to þe kynges consail as a kene baroun
> And knokked Consience in court bifore hem alle,
> And gert Goed Faith fle and Fals to abyde

77

And baldeliche baer adoun, with many a brihte noble,
Moche of þe wyt and wisdoem of Westministre halle.
He iogged til a iustice and iustede in his ere
And ouertulde al his treuthe with 'Taek this on amendement'

C.XXII.129-135

In the *Visio* Langland showed us what an ideal king could achieve;
here he shows us the bitter reality of what really went on.

Meanwhile Conscience is trying to enforce the law of *redde quod
debes* by making the Christians perform penance, since this is their
only real defence against sin. This law corresponds to the law of just
earning which Piers tried to enforce on his half-acre. Both laws
require men to accept justice (the one in 'mercede' for labour, the
other in their penance for sin); both offer men food and pardon
(C.VIII.69-70; IX.6-8; XXI.383-390). Together they comprise the
duty of the Christian subject. But neither Piers nor Conscience can
force their fellow-subjects to obey the law. At best they are only
backed up by natural forces (Hunger comes to Piers' aid; Kynde,
Elde, and Death to Conscience's). Piers only showed men how to
work by his own example, and there remained a proportion who
refused to follow it. Now Conscience can 'consail' the Christians to
pay their debts (XXI.391) and to shelter within *Unitas* (XXI.356,
XXII.74). Even this would be enough for those who do obey, for
Unitas seems able to withstand an indefinite siege, and to remain
under siege could be the most successful strategy in medieval warfare.[49] But Conscience has reckoned without the treason of his
closest supporters, the clergy. The monks have already been associated with the treason of forging false coin (XVII.72-84), and now it
is the friars who cause the fall of *Unitas*, just as it was one of God's
own knight-archangels who caused the Fall of Man.

Conscience is already rather wary of the friars, whom he accused
of being casual mercenaries in the battle with Antichrist. This situation disposes them to treason, for such mercenaries would not have
been entered on the indenture-rolls of the regular army, or be paid
the king's wages, but would have joined the army themselves in order
to share the plunder. This was forbidden by the Laws of War; indeed
when Edward III himself employed mercenaries in mid-campaign, he
had to sign special retrospective writs including them on his payroll
as if from the beginning.[50] By characterising the friars as illegal
mercenaries, Langland indicates that it is their freedom from discipline
and a regular stipend which makes them exploit their fellow-Christians
and eventually betray them:

'Kynges and knyhtes, þat kepen and defenden,
Haen officerys vnder hem and vch of hem a certeyne.
And yf thei wage men to werre thei writen hem in nombre; . . .

Alle oþere in bataile been yholde brybours,
Pilours and pike-harneys, in vch a parsch acorsed. . . .
Forthy,' quod Consience, 'bi Crist, kynde wit me telleth
Hit is wikked to wage ʒow, ʒe wexeth out of nombre.'

C.XXII.257-9, 262-3, 268-9

This passage might be directly inspired by one in *De Officio Regis*, in which Wycliffe also says that the numbers of the clergy should be limited, and that they should be controlled by their 'captains' lest they become thieves:

And therefore, just as the captains of the corporeal army must certify to the king the quantity and quality of their soldiers, as they correspond to the given stipends, so much more should the bishops, captains of the spiritual army, be responsible to the king for the numbers and the virtue of their spiritual soldiers . . . For . . . if such men take the goods of the kingdom, especially of the poor, being so much worse than common thieves and robbers that they are a source of harm to the whole realm, should not the king preserve . . . and defend his and his kingdom's goods from such enemies?[51]

Whereas Wycliffe gives the secular king the responsibility for restraining these corrupt elements within the Church, Langland gives this responsibility to Conscience alone.

The friars 'pillage the battlefield' by taking money from Christian soldiers in return for granting absolution for their sins without further penance. Such silver penances sooth the Christians' contrition for sin (allegorised here as wounds received in the battle), and replace the difficult repayment of what they owe to God and man, which only can earn Piers' pardon. This pillaging turns into treason when a friar disguises himself as a doctor and attempts to sell such penances within *Unitas* itself, to those Christians who have so far remained faithful. And since Conscience lacks final authority, or even the backing of Reason, he has to allow his 'subjects' to open the gates of besieged *Unitas*.

'Y may wel soffre,' sayde Consience, 'sennes ʒe desiren,
That frere Flaterare be fet and fisyk ʒow seke.'

C.XXII.322-3

Once inside the friar drugs the Christians' sense of sin and Sloth and Pride can enter *Unitas* and raise the siege. Since the friar is supposedly part of the Church, his surrender of the citadel while it is still garnished with supplies and soldiers[52] represents the supreme treason to Conscience. It is confirmed by the treason of nearly all who remain in *Unitas*, so that nothing is left of this society but its governor, Conscience. *Unitas* has utterly lost that of faithkeeping and harmony embodied in its name, and to which every kingdom in the poem had aspired.

Conscience is the least authoritative ruler in *Piers Plowman*, and his failure highlights the problem of obedience which confronts all the societies discussed by Langland. For all subjects and Christians are free men, and can choose whether they will follow their Consciences and create a 'relacoun rect' with their king or with God, or whether they will betray their own souls and their rulers. Conscience therefore does not go in search of the king whom he advised in the *Visio*, and who had — for a time — forced his subjects to obey Conscience. Such a monarch might be an ideal earthly ruler, but as a ruler of the Church he would condemn too many to everlasting damnation. Instead Conscience goes in search of Piers Plowman, the Pope who was also a subject-king, and who fed and cajoled his brother-Christians when they were Wasters on his half-acre. Only such a king or Pope might rule by example, as Christ did and, if his people fail to obey his law, might forgive and help them still.

CONCLUSION

Langland's political ideals are not inconsistent. They seem to change, depending on whether he is addressing the present king of England, or the subjects and Christians who are reading the poem. It is only parts of the Prologue and *Passus* II-IV which appear as a kind of 'Fürstenspiegel', a Mirror for Princes, in which England's governors are blamed for their weak tolerance of the over-powerful subject epitomized by Lady Meed or Wrong. But when similar problems are raised in the last two *Passus*, it is the individual Christians who are blamed for their own tolerance of Pride and Antichrist, their own treason to the Conscience who should rule all their actions. Then again, in the great allegories of the Atonement in *Passus* XVIII-XX, it is not Christ the King who is addressed, but the Christian reader. He can only wonder at Christ's obedience to the Old Law, epitomised by the laws of mainprise, charter, duel and pardon, and strive to obey Christ's New Law in return. Piers the Ploughman himself, whether tilling his half-acre or the whole of Christendom, is an ideal to be embraced not by kings and popes, but by fellow-ploughmen and subjects. If the king will not put England to rights, then it is the individual subject who must set about it, particularly as no king, not even Christ Himself, will take the responsibility for reforming man's free soul.

It would seem then that, like most 'political' poets of the time, Langland does not separate the political from the moral. When addressing the 'commune', this tends to make him a political conservative, teaching men to obey their own Consciences by keeping the laws, rather than (as the B-text Prologue implied) by helping the king to shape the laws. When addressing the king, Langland's reliance on the individual Conscience makes him hope for an absolute royal authority over both the subjects and the law, of a kind one would associate more with Edward I than with Edward III or the younger Richard II. In fact Langland's political ideals, both for the community and for the king, go counter to his own experience of law and government.

It seems to me that this is not because Langland was unaware of

81

contemporary political developments, but because he did not mean the *Visio* kingdom to be read simply as an analogy for English society. It is also an analogy for the society of the Church, in which the king is contrasted with Christ, and the labouring subjects are contrasted with Christians. The *Visio* king's successful assertion of justice over Meed and Wrong may in one sense be a model for Richard II. It is also a foil for Christ, who chooses not to judge Adam or his sinful descendants with the same severity, but instead to obey the conditions of the law on their behalf. Similarly, Piers' unwillingness to punish his own recalcitrant but free employees reflects Christ's refusal to force men to obey their Consciences. Viewed in this light it does not really matter that Lady Meed remained at large in Langland's own kingdom, or that labourers generally preferred to abuse their new-found freedoms. A poem is not a political programme, however firmly it is rooted in contemporary life. Only Christ can truly combine in His double nature the ideal subject who obeys the law, and the ideal king who overturns it in favour of a new kind of justice and mercy.

BIBLIOGRAPHY
(including abbreviations and cue-titles)

Texts of Piers Plowman

Quotations from the poem are made from the three following editions:

A-text	*'Piers the Plowman': a Critical Edition of the A-version*, ed. T. A. Knott & D. C. Fowler (Baltimore 1952)
B-text	*Piers Plowman: the B Version*, ed. G. Kane & E. T. Donaldson (London 1975)
C-text	*'Piers Plowman' by William Langland: an edition of the C-text*, ed. D. A. Pearsall (London 1978). This is the principal text used throughout

Reference is also made to the following editions:

Bennett *Piers Plowman*	Langland, W. *'Piers Plowman': the Prologue and Passus I-VII of the B-text*, ed. J. A. W. Bennett (Oxford 1972)
Goodridge	Langland, W. *Piers the Ploughman* (B-text) tr. J. F. Goodridge (Penguin, London 1966)

General Bibliography

Works are listed alphabetically, under the author or title of primary sources, and the author or editor of secondary sources. Cue-titles (which are also cross-referenced alphabetically) appear in the left-hand column, and abbreviations of periodicals etc. are included with them.

	Alford, J. A. 'Literature and law in Medieval England', *PMLA* xcii (1977) 941-951
Alford	Alford, J. A. 'Some unidentified quotations in *Piers Plowman*', *MP* lxxii (1974-5) 390-399
Allmand	Allmand, C. T. 'The war and the non-combatant', Fowler, 163-183
	The Apocryphal New Testament, ed. M. R. James (Oxford 1924)
Archiv	*Archiv fur das Studium der neuren Sprachen und Literaturer*
Sel. Pol. Writings	Aquinas, St. T. *Selected Political Writings*, ed. A. P. d'Entrèves, tr. G. Dawson (Oxford 1970): includes
De Reg. Princ.	*De Regimine Principium* Bk. I and parts of *S. T.*
S. T.	Aquinas, St. T. *Summa Theologica* (no particular ed. used)
	Ault, W. O. 'Some early village By-laws', *EHR* xlv (1930) 208-231

Ault, W. O. 'Manors and temporalities', Morris, iii, 3-34

Ault, W. O. *Open-field Farming in Medieval England* (London 1970)

Avery, M. E. 'The history of the equitable jurisdiction of the Chancery before 1400', *BIHR* xlii (1969) 129-144

BIHR   *Bulletin of the Institute of Historical Research*

Bacon, R. *Opera hactenus inedita Rogeri Baconi* v, ed. R. Steele (Oxford 1920)

Baldwin   Baldwin, J. F. *The King's Council in England during the Middle Ages* (Oxford 1913)

Balogh, J. 'Rex a recte regendo', *Speculum* iii (1928) 580-2

Barber, R. *The Knight and Chivalry* (London 1970)

Baum, P. E. 'The Fable of belling the cat', *MLN* xxxiv (1919) 462-470

Bayley, C. C. 'Pivotal concepts in the political philosophy of William of Ockham', *Journal of the History of Ideas* x (1949) 199-218

Bean, J. M. W. *The Decline of English Feudalism 1215-1540* (Manchester 1966)

Bellamy *Treason*   Bellamy, J. G. *The Law of Treason in England in the Late Middle Ages* (Cambridge 1970)

Bellamy *Crime*   Bellamy, J. *Crime and Public Order in England in the Later Middle Ages* (London 1973)

Bennett *Manor*   Bennett, H. S. *Life on the English Manor* (Cambridge 1937)

Bennett, 'Date of the B-text'   Bennett, J. A. W. 'The date of the B-text of *Piers Plowman*', *Med. Aev.* xii (1943) 55-64

Bennett *Piers Plowman*   see list of texts preceding General Bibliography

Bennett, J. W. 'The medieval loveday', *Speculum* xxxiii (1958) 351-370

Bergres, W. *Die Fürstenspiegel des hohen und späten Mittelalters* (Leipzig 1938)

Birdsall, P. '"Non obstante" — a study of the dispensing power of English Kings', *Essays in History and Political Theory in honour of C. H. McIlwain*, ed. C. Wittke (Harvard 1931) 37-76

Birnes, W. J. *Patterns of Legality in 'Piers Plowman'* (New York University Ph.D. thesis 1974)

Birnes, W. J. 'Christ as advocate: the legal metaphor in *Piers Plowman*', *Annuale Medievale* xvi (1975) 71-93

Black Book   *The Black Book of the Admiralty*, ed. T. Twiss (R.S. 55, 1871)

Blackstone   Blackstone, W. *Commentaries on the Laws of England* (1765, 3rd ed., Dublin 1770)

Bloch, M. *Feudal Society*, tr. M. A. Manyon (1940, 2nd ed., London 1962)

Bloomfield   Bloomfield, M. W. *'Piers Plowman' as a Fourteenth-Century Apocalypse* (New Brunswick 1961)

Tree of Battles   Bonet, H. *The Tree of Battles*, ed. and tr. G. W. Coopland (Liverpool 1949)

Born   Born, L. K. 'The perfect prince', *Speculum* iii (1928) 470-504

	Borough Customs ii, ed. M. Bateson (Seld. Soc. 21, 1906)
	Bowers, R. H. 'A Middle-English poem on lovedays', *MLR* xlvii (1952) 374-5
	Bozon, N. *An Allegorical Romance on the Death of Christ, The Chronicle of Pierre de Langtoft* (R.S. 47, 1868) ii, 427-447
	Bozon, N. *Les Contes Moralisés de Nichole Bozon*, ed. L. Toulmin Smith & P. Meyer (SATF 29, 1889)
Bracton	Bracton, H. *De Legibus et Consuetudinis Angliae*, ed. G. E. Woodbine tr. S. E. Thorne (Harvard 1968)
	Brett, E. 'Notes on Old and Middle English', *MLN* xxii (1927) 257-264
	Brinton, T. *The Sermons of Thomas Brinton*, ed. M. A. Devlin (Camd. Soc. 85-6, 1954)
	Brown, A. L. 'The authorization of letters under the Great Seal', *BIHR* xxxvii (1964) 125-155
Cal. Close Rolls	*Calendar of Close Rolls* (PRO 1892-)
Cal. Pat. Rolls	*Calendar of Patent Rolls* (PRO 1891-)
	Calendar of Letter Books in the City of London, ed. R. R. Sharpe (London 1899-1912)
	Calendar of Plea and Memorial Rolls 1364-1381, ed. A. H. Thomas (London 1929)
Cam *Liberties*	Cam, H. M. *Liberties and Communities in Medieval England* (Cambridge 1944)
	Cam, H. M. 'Shire officials: coroners, constables and bailiffs', Morris iii, 143-183
Camd. Soc.	Camden Society
Carlyle	Carlyle, R. W. & A. J. *A History of Medieval Political Theory in the West* (London 1903-36)
Cases in Chancery	see *Select Cases in Chancery*
Cases before Council	see *Select Cases before the King's Council*
	Catto, J. 'Ideas and experience in the political thought of Aquinas', *P & P* lxxi (1976) 3-31
	Chadwick, D. *Social Life in the Days of 'Piers Plowman'* (Cambridge 1922)
	Chrimes, S. B. *English Constitutional Ideas in the Fifteenth Century* (Cambridge 1936)
Chroust	Chroust, A. H. 'The corporate idea and the body politic in the Middle Ages', *Review of Politics* ix (1947) 423-452
	Cohn, N. *The Pursuit of the Millennium* (1957, Paladin, 1970)
Confessio Amantis	see Gower, J.
	Corpus Iuris Civilis, ed. P. Krueger et al. (Weidmannos 1840-1939)
	Corville, A. 'France: the Hundred Years' War', *Cambridge Medieval History*, ed. J. C. Tanner et al. (Cambridge 1932) 340-367
	Cowell, J. *The Interpreter* (Cambridge 1607)
	Cripps-Day, F. H. *The History of the Tournament* (London 1918)
Crowned King	*Crowned King, Historical Poems*, 227-232
	Davenport, F. G. *The Economic Development of a Norfolk Manor* (London 1906)

Dawson	Dawson, C. *Medieval Essays* (London 1953)
De Bello	see Legnano, G. de
De Offic. Reg.	see Wyclif, J.
	Devlin, M. A. 'The date of the C-version of *Piers the Plowman*', *Abstracts of Theses, Univ. of Chicago, Humanistic Ser.* iv (1925-6) 317-320
Digby MS	see *Twenty-six Political and Other Poems*
	Dicey, A. V. *The Privy Council* (London 1887)
	Dobson, R. B. *The Peasants' Revolt of 1381* (London 1970)
Donaldson	Donaldson, E. T. *'Piers Plowman': the C-text and its Poet* (New Haven 1949)
Du Boulay	Du Boulay, F. R. H. & Barron, C. M. (eds) *The Reign of Richard II* (London 1971)
	Dugdale, W. *Origines Juridicales* (London 1660)
Dunning	Dunning, T. E. *'Piers Plowman': an Interpretation of the A-text* (Torono 1937)
EETS	Early English Text Society
EHR	*The English Historical Review*
Econ. Hist. Rev.	*Economic History Review*
Edwards	Edwards, J. G. et al. (eds) *Historical Essays in Honour of James Tait* (Manchester 1933)
	Eliason, M. 'The peasant and the lawyer', *S in P* xlviii (1951) 506-526
	d'Entrèves, A.P. *Natural Law* (1951, 2nd edn., London 1970)
Farr	Farr, W. *John Wyclif as Legal Reformer* (Leiden 1974)
	Ferguson, A. B. 'The problem of counsel in *Mum and the Sothsegger*', *Studies in the Renaissance* ii (1955) 67-83
	Figgis, J. M. *The Divine Right of Kings* (1896, 2nd ed., London 1914)
	Fleta, ed. H. G. Richardson & G. O. Sayles (Seld. Soc. 72, 1953/5)
	Ford, B. (ed.) *The Age of Chaucer* (Pelican, 1954)
	Fortescue, J. *De Laudibus Legum Anglie* ed. and tr. S. B. Chrimes (Cambridge 1949)
	Four English Political Tracts of the Later Middle Ages, ed. J. P. Genet (Camd. Soc. 4th ser., 1977)
Fowler	Fowler, K. (ed.) *The Hundred Years' War* (London 1971)
	Fryde, E. B. & Miller, E. (eds) *Historical Studies of the English Parliament* (Cambridge 1970)
	Galbraith, V. H. 'Articles laid before the Parliament of 1371', *EHR* xxxiv (1919) 579-582
Gierke	Gierke, O. *Political Theories of the Middle Age*, tr. F. W. Maitland (Cambridge 1922)
	Gilbert, A. H. *Machiavelli's 'Prince' and its Forerunners* (Duke Univ. 1938)
	Glanvill *The Treatise of the Laws and Customs of England commonly called Glanvill*, ed. G. D. G. Hall (London 1965)
Confessio Amantis	Gower, J. *Confessio Amantis*, ed. J. C. Macaulay (EETS es 81-2, 1900-1)
	Gratian *Decretum*
	Haas, E. de *Antiquities of Bail* (Columbia 1940)

HMSO	Her Majesty's Stationery Office
Hale	Hale, M. *The Jurisdiction of the Lords' House* (London, ed. of 1796)
Harding	Harding, A. *The Law Courts of Medieval England* (London 1973)
Hastings	Hastings, M. *The Court of Common Pleas in Fifteenth Century England* (Cornell 1947)
	Hay, D. 'The division of the spoils of war in fourteenth-century England', *TRHS* 5th ser., iv (1954) 91-109
Hewitt	Hewitt, H. G. *The Organisation of War under Edward III, 1338-62* (Manchester 1966)
	Hilton, R. H. *The Decline of Serfdom in Medieval England* (London 1969)
	Hilton, R. H. *The English Peasantry in the Later Middle Ages* (Oxford 1975)
Hist Poems	*Historical Poems of the Fourteenth and Fifteenth Centuries*, ed. R. H. Robbins (New York 1959): includes *Crowned King*
Reg. Princes	Hoccleve, T. *The Regement of Princes*, ed. F. J. Furnivall (EETS es 72, 1897)
Holdsworth	Holdsworth, W. *A History of English Law*, i (4th ed., London 1927), ii (4th ed., 1936), iii (5th ed., 1942)
	Hort, G. *'Piers Plowman' and Contemporary Religious Thought* (London 1938)
	Huppé, B. 'The A-text of *Piers Plowman* and the Norman Wars', *PMLA* liv (1939) 37-64
	Huppé, B. 'The date of the B-text of *Piers Plowman*', *S in P* xxxviii (1941) 34-44
Hurnard	Hurnard, N. D. *The King's Pardon for Homicide before 1307* (Oxford 1969)
Hussey	Hussey, S. S. (ed.) *'Piers Plowman': Critical Approaches* (London 1969)
JEGP	*The Journal of English and German Philology*
Jacob	Jacob, G. *A New Law Dictionary* (London 1729)
Jenkins	Jenkins, P. 'Conscience: the frustration of allegory', Hussey, 125-142
	Jusserand, J. J. *English Wayfaring Life in the Middle Ages (XIVth Century)*, tr. L. T. Smith (1889, 3rd ed., London 1894)
Jusserand *Piers Plowman*	Jusserand, J. J. *'Piers Plowman': a Contribution to the History of English Mysticism*, tr. M. E. R. (2nd ed., London 1894)
	Imray, J. M. 'Les Bones Gentes de la Mercerys de Londres', *Studies in London History presented to P. E. Jones*, ed. A. E. J. Hollaender & W. Kellaway (London 1969) 155-178
Kantorowicz	Kantorowicz. E. H. *The King's Two Bodies* (Princeton 1957)
Kean 'Love'	Kean, P. H. 'Love, law and *lewte* in *Piers Plowman*', *RES* ns. xv (1964) 241-261
	Kean, P. H. 'Justice, kingship and the good life in the second part of *Piers Plowman*', Hussey, 76-110
Keen 'Treason trials'	Keen, M. 'Treason trials under the Law of Arms', *TRHS* 5th ser. xii (1962) 85-104

	Keen, M. H. 'Brotherhood in Arms', *History* xlvii (1962) 1-17
Keen *Laws*	Keen, M. H. *The Laws of War in the Late Middle Ages* (London 1965)
	Kellogg, E. H. 'Bishop Brunton and the fable of the rats', *PMLA* 1 (1935) 57-68
Kerly	Kerly, D. M. *A Historical Sketch of the Equitable Jurisdiction of the Court of Chancery* (Cambridge 1890)
	Kirk, R. 'References to the law in *Piers Plowman*', *PMLA* xlviii (1933) 327-377
	Langland, W. *Piers Plowman*: texts used are listed before the General Bibliography
	Lawlor, J. *'Piers Plowman': an Essay in Criticism* (London 1962)
Legg	Legg, L. G. W. *English Coronation Records* (London 1901)
De Bello	Legnano, G. de *Tractatus de Bello, de Represaliis et de Duello*, ed. T. Holland (Oxford 1917)
Lewis 'Organic tendencies'	Lewis, E. 'Organic tendencies in medieval political thought', *American Political Science Review* xxxii (1938) 849-876
	Lewis, E. 'Natural Law and expediency in medieval political theory', *Ethics* 1 (1939) 144-163
MLN	*Modern Language Notes*
MP	*Modern Philology*
	Maitland, F. W. 'The history of a Cambridgeshire manor', *EHR* ix (1894) 417-439
Maitland *'Mem. de Parliamento'*	Maitland, F. W. 'Introduction to *Memoranda de Parliamento*', *Historical Studies of the English Parliament*, ed. E. B. Fryde & E. Miller (Cambridge 1970)
	Mann, J. *Chaucer and Medieval Estates Satire* (Cambridge 1973)
Mathew 'Justice'	Mathew, G. 'Justice and charity in *The Vision of Piers Plowman*', *Dominican Studies* i (1948) 360-365
	Mathew, G. *The Court of Richard II* (London 1968)
	Maxwell-Lyte, H. C. *Historical Notes on the Use of the Great Seal of England* (HMSO 1926)
	McFarlane, K. B. ' "Bastard feudalism" ', *BIHR* xx (1943-5) 161-180
McFarlane *Nobility*	McFarlane, K. B. *The Nobility of Later Medieval England* (1953, Oxford 1973)
McKisack	McKisack, M. *The Fourteenth Century* (Oxford History of England v, Oxford 1959)
Med. Aev.	*Medium Aevum*
	Milsom, S. F. C. *Historical Foundations of the Common Law* (London 1969)
MED	*Middle English Dictionary*
Mirror of Justices	*The Mirror of Justices*, ed. W. J. Whittaker (Seld. Soc. 7, 1895)
Mitchell	Mitchell, A. G. *Lady Meed and the Art of 'Piers Plowman'* (Chambers Memorial Lecture, London 1956)
	Mohl, R. *The Three Estates in Medieval and Renaissance Literature* (Columbia 1973)
Morris	Morris, W. A. et al. (eds) *The English Government at Work 1327-1336* (Medieval Academy of America 1940-1950)

Morris, W. 'The Sheriff', Morris ii, 41-108

Mum   *Mum and the Sothsegger*, ed. M. Day & R. Steele (EETS os 199, 1936)

N & Q   *Notes and Queries*

Neilson, G. *Trial by Combat* (Glasgow 1890)

OED   *Oxford English Dictionary*

Ordinances of War   *Ordinances of War made by King Richard II at Durham, Ao 1385, Black Book* i, 353-8

Owen   Owen, D. *'Piers Plowman': a Comparison with some Earlier and Contemporary French Allegories* (London 1912)

Owst   Owst, G. R. *Literature and Pulpit in Medieval England* (Oxford 1933)

PMLA   *Publications of the Modern Language Association of America*

P & P   *Past and Present*

PRO   Public Record Office

Palgrave, F. *As Essay on the Original Authority of the King's Council* (Record Commission 1834)

Palmer, J. 'The war aims of the protagonists and the negotiations for peace', Fowler, 5-74

Pearsall *Piers*   see list of texts preceding General Bibliography
Plowman

Plucknett, T. F. T. 'The origin of impeachment', *TRHS* 4th ser. xxiv (1942) 47-71

Pol. Poems   *Political Poems and Songs*, ed. T. Wright (R.S. 14, 1859, 1861)

Pol. Songs   *The Political Songs of England*, ed. T. Wright (Camd. Soc. 6, 1839)

Pollock, F. 'The history of the Law of Nature', *Journal of the Society of Comparative Legislation* ns ii (1900) 418-433

Pollock & Maitland   Pollock, F. & Maitland, F. W. *The History of English Law before the Time of Edward I* (1895, 2nd edn., Cambridge 1968)

Post   Post, G. *Studies in Medieval Legal Thought* (Princeton 1964)

Postan 'Consequences   Postan, M. M. 'Some social consequences of the Hundred of war'   Years' War', *Econ. Hist. Rev.* xii (1942) 1-12

Postan, M. M. 'The costs of the Hundred Years' War', *P & P* xxvii (1964) 34-53

Powicke   Powicke, M. 'The English aristocracy and the war', Fowler, 122-134

Prince 'Indenture   Prince, A. E. 'The indenture system under Edward III', system'   Edwards, 283-297

Prince, A. E. 'The payment of army wages in Edward III's reign', *Speculum* xix (1944) 137-160

Pugh, R. B. *Imprisonment in Medieval England* (Cambridge 1968)

Putnam   Putnam, B. *The Enforcement of the Statutes of Labourers during the First Decade after the Black Death, 1349-59* (Columbia 1908)

Quirk, R. 'Langland's use of Kynde Wit and Inwit', *JEGP* lii (1953) 182-188

RES   *The Review of English Studies*

R.S. Rolls Series

Reeves, M. 'Joachist influences in the idea of a last world Emperor', *Traditio* xvii (1961)

Reg. Brev. *Registrum Omnium Brevium* (London 1531)

Richardson, H. G. *The English Jewry under Angevin Kings* (London 1960)

Robertson, D. W. & Huppé, B. F. *'Piers Plowman' and Scriptural Tradition* (Princeton 1951)

Roth, C. *A History of the Jews in England* (Oxford 1941)

Rot. Parl. *Rotuli Parliamentorum*, ed. J. Strachey (London 1767-1777) ii & iii

SATF Société des Anciens Textes Français

S in P *Studies in Philology*

St. Jacques, R. 'Langland's Christ-knight and the liturgy', *Rev. Univ. Ottowa* xxxvii (1967) 146-158

Sajavaara, K. (ed.) *The Middle English Translations of Robert Grosseteste's 'Chateau d'Amour'* (Mémoires de la Société Néophilologique de Helsinki 23, 1967)

Salter, E. '*Piers Plowman* and the *Simonie*', *Archiv* cciii (1967) 241-254

The Sarum Missal, ed. J. W. Legg (Oxford 1916)

Schmidt, A. V. 'Langland and scholastic philosophy', *Med. Aev.* xxxviii (1969) 134-156

Schramm Schramm, P. E. *A History of the English Coronation*, tr. L. G. W. Legg (Oxford 1937)

Schroeder, M. C. 'The character of Conscience in Piers Plowman', *S in P* lxvii (1970) 13-30

Schulz Schulz, F. 'Bracton on kingship', *EHR* lx (1945) 136-176

Secreta *Three Prose Versions of the 'Secreta Secretorum'*, ed. R. Steele & T. Henderson (EETS os 30, 1867)

Sel. Pol. Writings see Aquinas, St. T.

Selden, J. *The Dvello or Single Combat* (London 1610)

Seld. Soc. Selden Society

Cases in Chancery *Select Cases in Chancery 1364-1471*, ed. W. P. Baildon (Seld. Soc. 10, 1896)

Select Cases in the Court of King's Bench under Edward III vi, ed. G. O. Sayles (Seld. Soc. 82, 1965)

Cases before Council *Select Cases before the King's Council 1243-1482*, ed. L. S. Leadam & J. F. Baldwin (Seld. Soc. 35, 1918)

The Simonie, Pol. Songs, 323-345

Simpson Simpson, A. W. B. *An Introduction to the History of the Land Law* (Oxford 1961)

Song of Lewes *The Song of Lewes*, ed. C. L. Kingsford (Oxford 1890)

Spalding, M. C. *The Middle English Charters of Christ* (Bryn Mawr 1914)

Squibb, G. D. *The High Court of Chivalry* (Oxford 1959)

Stat. Realm *The Statutes of the Realm* (London 1810, 1816) i & ii

Steele, A. 'English government finance, 1377-1413', *EHR* li (1936) 29-51, 577-597

Stones, E. C. 'The Folvilles of Ashby-Folville, Leicestershire, and their associates in crime, 1326-1347', *TRHS* 5th ser. vii (1957) 117-136

Storey   Storey, R. L. 'Liveries and Commissions of the Peace', Du Boulay, 131-152

TRHS   *Transactions of the Royal Historical Society*

Taylor, R. *The Political Prophecy in England* (Columbia 1911)

Tout   Tout, T. F. *Chapters in the Administrative History of Medieval England* (Manchester 1920-33)

Traver, H. *The Four Daughters of God* (Bryn Mawr Monographs 6, 1907)

Tuck 'Patronage'   Tuck, J. A. 'Richard II's system of patronage', Du Boulay, 1-20

Tuck *Richard II*   Tuck, A. *Richard II and the English Nobility* (London 1973)

Tucker, S. M. *Verse Satire in England before the Renaissance* (New York 1961)

Digby MS   *Twenty-six Political and Other Poems (from Bodleian MS Digby 102)*, ed. J. Kail (EETS os 124, 1904)

Ullmann   Ullmann, W. *A History of Political Thought: the Middle Ages* (rev. ed., Pelican 1970)

Walter of Henley and other Treatises on Estates Management and Accounting, ed. D. Oschinsky (Oxford 1971)

Whitworth, C. W. 'Changes in the roles of Reason and Conscience in the revisions of Piers Plowman', *N & Q* ccxvii (1972) 4-7

Wilkinson, B. *The Chancery under Edward III* (Manchester 1929)

Wilkinson, B. 'The Coronation Oath of Edward II', Edwards, 405-416

Wilkinson, B. *Constitutional History of Medieval England*, ii (London 1952)

Winfield   Winfield, P. H. *The History of Conspiracy and Abuse of Legal Procedure* (Cambridge 1921)

Wolffe, B. P. *The Royal Demesne in English History* (London 1974)

Wyclif *Engl. Works*   Wyclif, J. *The English Works of Wyclif*, ed. F. D. Matthew (EETS os 74, 1880, 2nd. ed. 1902)

Wyclif, J. *Fasculi Zizanorum Magistri Johannis Wyclif*, ed. W. W. Shirley (R.S. 5, 1898)

De Offic. Reg.   Wyclif, J. *Tractatus de Officio Regis*, ed. A. W. Pollard & C. Sayle (Wyclif Soc. 1887)

Yunck   Yunck, J. A. *The Lineage of Lady Meed* (Notre Dame, Indiana 1963)

NOTES

Introduction

[1] References, unless otherwise stated, are to *'Piers Plowman' by William Langland: an edition of the C-text*, ed. D. Pearsall (London 1978).

[2] J. J. Jusserand, *'Piers Plowman': a contribution to the History of English Mysticism*, tr. M. E. R. (London 1894), p.106, and see 103-125.

[3] R. H. Hilton, *The English Peasantry in the Later Middle Ages* (Oxford 1975), 20-22; D. Chadwick, *Social Life in the Days of Piers Plowman* (Cambridge 1922); see also S. M. Tucker, *Verse Satire in England before the Renaissance* (New York 1966), 70-79; C. Dawson, *Medieval Essays* (London 1953), 239-271.

[4] G. Mathew, 'Justice and Charity in *The Vision of Piers Plowman'*, *Dominican Studies* i (1948), 360-5, p.363.

[5] E. T. Donaldson, *'Piers Plowman': the C-text and its Poet* (New Haven 1949), 85-120 (see bibliography of political commentaries on the poem, p.85 n.1); M. W. Bloomfield, *'Piers Plowman' as a Fourteenth-Century Apocalypse* (New Brunswick 1961); J. Lawlor, *'Piers Plowman': an Essay in Criticism* (London 1962); R. Kirk, 'References to the Law in *Piers Plowman'*, *PMLA* xlviii (1933), 327-377; G. Mathew, 'Justice'; M. Eliason, 'The peasant and the lawyer', *S in P* xlviii (1951) 506-526; P. M. Kean, 'Love, law and *lewte* in *Piers Plowman'*, *RES* ns.xv (1964) 241-261; 'Justice, kingship and the good life in the second part of *Piers Plowman'*, *'Piers Plowman': critical approaches*, ed. S. S. Hussey (London 1969), 76-110; W. J. Birnes, 'Christ as advocate: the legal metaphor in *Piers Plowman'*, *Annuale Medievale* xvi (1975), 71-93; J. A. Alford, 'Literature and law in medieval England', *PMLA* xcii (1977), 941-951.

[6] M. A. Devlin, 'The date of the C-version of *Piers the Plowman'*, *Abstracts of theses, Univ. of Chicago, Humanistic Ser.* iv (1925-6), 317-320 (cited Donaldson, 19); J. A. W. Bennett, 'The date of the B-text of *Piers Plowman'*, *Med. Aev.* xii (1943), 55-64. B-text references are taken from *'Piers Plowman': the B Version*, ed. G. Kane & E. T. Donaldson (London 1975).

Chapter I   The problem of authority

[1] E. Lewis, 'Organic tendencies in medieval political thought', *American Political Science Review* xxxii (1938), 849-876, pp.864-5; see also A. H. Chroust, 'The corporate idea and the body politic in the Middle Ages', *Review of Politics* ix (1947), 423-452.

[2] J. Gower, *Confessio Amantis*, ed. G. C. Macaulay (EETS es. 81-2, 1900-1) I, 106-110.

3 *Three prose versions of the 'Secreta Secretorum'*, ed. R. Steele & T. Henderson (EETS os. 30, 1867), 143, cp. *Opera hactenus inedita Rogeri Baconi* v, ed. R. Steele (Oxford 1920), 57; see also *Mum and the Sothsegger*, ed. M. Day & R. Steele (EETS os. 199, 1936) I, ll. 32-48; *Political poems and songs*, ed. T. Wright (R.S. 14, 1859, 1861) i, 355: 'Cessat justitia, cessatque fides societa'; T. Hoccleve, *The Regement of Princes*, ed. F. J. Furnivall (EETS es. 72, 1897), ll. 2211-2, 2402-2415; *Confessio Amantis* VII, ll. 1723-1774. On lewte, see below n. 25.

4 On Langland's place in this tradition, see R. Mohl, *The three estates in medieval and renaissance literature* (Columbia 1933), 103-5; J. Mann, *Chaucer and medieval estates satire* (Cambridge 1973), 191-2, 208-212; G. R. Owst, *Literature and pulpit in medieval England* (Oxford 1933), 549-575; Jusserand, 115-122; T. F. Dunning, *'Piers Plowman': an interpretation of the A-text* (Toronto 1937), 129-132.

5 L. K. Born, 'The perfect prince', *Speculum* iii (1928), 470-504; A. H. Gilbert, *Machiavelli's 'Prince' and its forerunners* (Duke Univ. 1938), 3-15; A. B. Ferguson, 'The problem of counsel in *Mum and the Sothsegger'*, *Studies in the renaissance*, ii (1955), 67-83; Bloomfield, 110; W. Berges, *Die Fürstenspiegel des hohen und späten Mittelalters* (Leipzig 1938).

6 J. Wyclif, *Tractatus de Officio Regis*, ed. A. W. Pollard & C. Sayle (Wyclif Soc. 1887); *Twenty-six political and other poems (from Bodleian MS Digby 102)*, ed. J. Kail (EETS os. 124, 1904); for *Richard Redeless* see *Mum*, 1-26; for *Crowned King*, see *Historical poems of the fourteenth and fifteenth centuries*, ed. R. H. Robbins (New York 1959), 227-232; see n. 3 above.

7 *Walter of Henley and other treatises on estates management and accounting*, ed. D. Oschinsky (Oxford 1971), 312-3, 394-5, 434-7; H. S. Bennett, *Life on the English Manor* (Cambridge 1937), 186-192; cp. C. XI. 299-301.

8 J. M. Figgis, *The Divine Right of Kings* (1896, 2nd. ed. London 1914), 38-65; E. H. Kantorowicz, *The King's Two Bodies* (Princeton 1957), 78-86, 127-135; W. Ullmann, *A History of Political Thought: the Middle Ages* (rev. ed. Pelican 1970), 32-38, 130-145. For Civil Law quotations, see *Corpus Iuris Civilis*, ed. P. Krueger et al. (Weidmannos 1840-1939), *Institutes*, 1:2:6, *Digest*, 1:4:1, *Code*, 1:14:4, *Novel*, 105:2:4.

9 *Rot. Parl.* III, 420b, tr. B. Wilkinson, *Constitutional History of Medieval England*, ii (London 1952), p. 395; R. Tuck, *Richard II and the English Nobility* (London 1973), 209-210.

10 *Summa Theologica* IIa-IIae.q.lxvi, a. 7 (see also a. 8 and q.lxxvii-lxxviii) cited E. Lewis, 'Natural law and expediency in medieval political theory', *Ethics* l (1939-40), 144-163; see also Gratian, *Decretum*, I dist. vii, V dist. xli. 4. For a different discussion of Need, see Bloomfield, 135-143.

11 V. H. Galbraith, 'Articles laid before the Parliament of 1371', *EHR* xxxiv (1919), 579-582; C. C. Bayley, 'Pivotal concepts in the political philosophy of William of Ockham', *Journal of the History of Ideas*, x (1949), 199-218; W. Farr, *John Wyclif as Legal Reformer* (Leiden 1974), 142-5; G. Post, *Studies in Medieval Legal Thought* (Princeton 1964), 253-309. See also *Fasculi Zizanorum Magistri Johannis Wyclif*, ed. W. W. Shirley (R.S. 5, 1898), 254-271.

12 Kantorowicz, 105-6, see also 87-143 *passim.*; O. Gierke, *Political Theories of the Middle Age*, tr. F. W. Maitland (Cambridge 1922), 73-82; R. W. & A. J. Carlyle, *A History of Medieval Political Theory in the West* (London 1903-36) v, 64-106, vi, 74-86.

13 *De Offic. Reg.*, 97, see also 118-145; Farr, 144-7, 150-153; Carlyle, vi, 51-63. Like Wyclif (see e.g. *De Offic. Reg.*, 213) Langland even suggests that the

king should take away all the Church's temporalities (C.V.168-179). For later tracts developing absolutist theories of this kind, see *Four English Political Tracts of the Later Middle Ages*, ed. J. P. Genet (Camd. Soc. 4th ser. 1977).

14 *De Offic. Reg.*, 93; cp. *Digby MS*, 9-14, *Pol. Poems* ii, 238; see Kantorowicz, 48-9.

15 J. Fortescue, *De Laudibus Legum Anglie*, ed. and tr. S. B. Chrimes (Cambridge 1949), xiii-xiv, xlvii-xlviii, Ch.XXV-XXVI; S. B. Chrimes, *English Constitutional Ideas of the Fifteenth Century* (Cambridge 1936), 300-341; Carlyle vi, 30-37; Ullmann, 145-158; P. Birdsall, ' "Non obstante" — a study of the dispensing power of English kings', 37-76 in *Essays in History and Political Theory in Honour of C. H. McIlwain*, ed. C. Wittke (Harvard 1936), 55-8, 62-3; and see below Ch.II n.41.

16 Donaldson, 85-120 (giving 'Coronation' evidence also); see also E. Brett, 'Notes on Old and Middle English', *MLN* xxii (1927), 257-264; Owst, 575-589; Bloomfield, 109-110; Bennett, 'Date of the B-text'; Kean, 'Love', 241-7.

17 'Since a king is entitled to be a king only by the act of ruling, he is a king only in name if he does not maintain the laws' (W. Langland, *Piers the Ploughman (B-text)*, tr. J. F. Goodridge (Penguin, London 1966), 29).

18 'The king's decrees are as binding to us as the Law' (Goodridge, 29); see J. A. Alford, 'Some unidentified quotations in *Piers Plowman*', *MP* lxxii (1974-5), 390-9.

19. Printed in L. G. W. Legg, *English Coronation Records* (London 1901), 3-13, 30-42, 81-130; see P. E. Schramm, *A History of the English Coronation*, tr. L. G. W. Legg (Oxford 1937), 78-88, 203-213.

20 *Bracton de Legibus et Consuetudinis Angliae*, ed. G. E. Woodbine, tr. S. E. Thorne (Harvard 1968), 304-306 (ff.107-8, and see ff.5-6); discussed F. Schulz, 'Bracton on kingship', *EHR* lx (1945), 136-176; Kantorowicz, 143-192. On Bracton, see W. Holdsworth, *A History of English Law*, ii (4th ed., London 1936), 236-243.

21 Legg, 88 (Donaldson, 106); Schramm, 203-213; B. Wilkinson, 'The Coronation Oath of Edward II', pp.405-416 in *Historical Essays in Honour of James Tait*, ed. J. C. Edwards et al. (Manchester 1933).

22 See J. Balogh, 'Rex a recte regendo', *Speculum*, iii (1928), 580-582; Schulz, 151-3; Born, 474; Alford, 391-2.

23 *The Song of Lewes*, ed. C. L. Kingsford (Oxford 1890), ll.871-2 (tr. 'It is commonly said, "As the king wills, the law goes"; truth wills otherwise, for the law stands, the king falls.')

24 *Pol. Poems* i, 278 (tr. 'O king, if you are king, rule yourself, or you will be a king without the essential of kingship; you will be a king only in name unless you rule rightly.'); see also i, 363.

25 *MED*: LEAUTE; *OED*: LAWTY, LEWTY: see Bloomfield, 166; Kean, 'Love', 254-7.

26 Tr. 'You say, "I am a king; I am a prince," — but in time you may be neither. It is your duty to administer the laws of Christ the King; the better to do this, be as mild as you are just.' (Goodridge, 29).

27 Bracton, 304; see Bloomfield, 210 n.33; Schulz p.137.

28 *De Regimine Principium* Ch.XII, p.67 in Aquinas, *Selected Political Writings*, ed. A. P. d'Entrèves, tr. G. Dawson (Oxford 1970); see Lewis, 'Organic Tendencies', 855-8; J. Catto, 'Ideas and experience in the political thought of Aquinas', *P & P* lxxi (1976), 3-21.

29 Baldus, *Commentary on Digest*, fol.10v, quoted Carlyle, vi, 82 n.1; Kantorowicz, 135.

30 *S.T.*, Ia, a.lxxix; see G. Hort, *'Piers Plowman' and Contemporary Religious Thought* (London 1938), 60-87; R. Quirk, 'Langland's use of Kynde Wit and Inwit', *JEGP* lii (1953), 182-8; Bloomfield, 111-2, 167-9; A. V. Schmidt, 'Langland and scholastic philosophy', *Med. Aev.* xxxviii (1969), 134-156; M. C. Schroeder, 'The character of Conscience in *Piers Plowman*', *S in P* lxvii (1970), 13-30; Dunning, 36-40, 99-101; C. W. Whitworth, 'Changes in the roles of Reason and Conscience in the revisions of *Piers Plowman*', *N & Q* ccxvii (1972), 4-7.

31 *Les Contes moralisés de Nichole Bozon*, ed. L. Toulmin Smith & P. Meyer (SATF, Paris 1889), 143-4; *The Sermons of Thomas Brinton*, ed. M. A. Devlin (Camd. Soc. lxxxv-lxxxvi, 1954), 317; discussed Jusserand, *Piers Plowman*, 39-48; D. L. Owen, *'Piers Plowman': a Comparison with some Earlier and Contemporary French Allegories* (London 1912), 86-7; P. F. Baum, 'The fable of belling the cat', *MLN* xxxiv (1919), 462-470; E. H. Kellogg, 'Bishop Brunton and the fable of the rats', *PMLA* L (1935), 57-68; B. Huppé, 'The date of the B-text of *Piers Plowman*', *S in P* xxxviii (1941), 34-44; and see n.16 above.

32 See Langland, *'Piers Plowman': the Prologue and Passus I-VII of the B-text*, ed. J. A. W. Bennett (Oxford 1972), n. to Prol.161-2; see infra Ch.II.

33 I have followed Skeat's reading here, as Langland must be referring to the boundary-marks between ploughlands (see Bennett, *Manor*, 48).

34 *Mum*, I ll.9-19 *passim.*; see also *Pol. Poems* ii, 4-5; *Reg. Princes*, ll.2777-9; *Hist. Poems*, 50-55.

35 Discussed Bloomfield, 112-4, see also 9, 109, 121-6.

36 T. F. T. Plucknett, 'The origin of impeachment', *TRHS* 4th ser. xxiv (1942), 47-71, see pp.56-7; the record of the king, coroners, and later J.P.s was 'enough to hang a man' (see *Stat. Realm* 15 Rich.II c.2). See also C.I.90-4 where kings and knights are told to take tresspassers to be tried by *'Treuthe'* and cp. *Stat. Realm* 34 Edw.III c.1 where J.P.s (often knights) are told to 'arrest [offenders] . . . and to cause them to be . . . duly punished according to the *Law*.'

37 *Patrologia Latina*, cxiv, 44-5, 58 (*Glossa Ordinaria*); cp. *Mum*, I, ll.352-371 (p.22-3); *Hist. Poems*, 113-117; *Song of Lewes*, ll.715-720; *Prol. Poems*, I, 203-6, 366-8, II, 1-4; see R. Taylor, *The political prophecy in England* (Columbia 1911), 90-8; N. Cohn, *The Pursuit of the Millennium* (1957, Paladin 1970); M. Reeves, 'Joachist influences in the idea of a last world Emperor', *Traditio* xvii (1961).

38 See n.30 above, in particular Schroeder, Whitworth, and P. Jenkins, 'Conscience: the frustration of allegory', pp.125-142 in Hussey.

39 *S.T.* Ia-IIae.q.91 a.2 (*Sel. Pol. Writings*, 114-5, see also 123-7); cp. *De Reg. Princ.* Ch.V (*ibid.* 224-7); *Digest*, 1:1:1; A. P. d'Entrèves, *Natural Law* (1951, 2nd. ed., London 1970), 42-49; Gierke, 74-76.

40 F. Pollock, 'The history of the Law of Nature', *Journal of the Society of Comparative Legislation*, n.s. ii (1900), 418-433 (giving St German and *Year Book* refs.); Holdsworth ii, 602-4; *Borough Customs* ii, ed. M. Bateson (Seld. Soc. 21, 1906), 59.

41 *Mum*, III, 207-243, IV, *M*, 99-205; *Digby MS*, 55-60; *Crowned King*; *Pol. Poems* ii, 238-247.

42 *Rot. Parl.* iii, 297a-298a (see D. M. Kerly, *A Historical Sketch of the Equitable Jurisdiction of the Court of Chancery* (Cambridge 1890), 40; see below Ch. III nn.8-10.

Chapter II   Lady Meed: the threat to authority

1   D. W. Robertson & B. F. Huppé, *'Piers Plowman' and Scriptural Tradition* (Princeton 1951), 49-71; A. G. Mitchell, *Lady Meed and the art of 'Piers Plowman'* (Chambers Memorial Lecture, London 1956); Dawson, 252; J. A. Yunck, *The Lineage of Lady Meed* (Notre Dame, Indiana 1963), 112-117, 285-306, 311-323.

2   *The Simonie* (or *On the evil times of Edward II*), pp. 323-345 in *The Political Songs of England*, ed. T. Wright (Camd. Soc. 6, 1839), ll. 241-288 and see E. Salter, *'Piers Plowman* and the *Simonie'*, *Archiv* cciii (1967), 241-254; *Wynnere and Wastoure*, ed. I. Gollancz, pp. 313-331 in *The Age of Chaucer*, ed. B. Ford (Pelican 1954), e.g. ll. 193-6, 423-438 etc.; see also *Pol. Songs*, 149-152, 237-240; *Pol. Poems* ii, 235-7; *Hist. Poems*, 127-130, 134-9, 149-150; *Digby MS*, 9-14, 25-7, 36, 55-60.

3   *Pol. Poems* ii, 238-242; see *Reg. Princes*, ll. 2787-2842; Jusserand, *Piers Plowman*, 187.

4   *Digby MS*, 6-9, ll. 49-50; see also *Crowned King*, ll. 85-92; *Secreta*, 52-3, 161; *Pol. Poems* i, 270-8, 361-6; *Hist. Poems*, 203-5.

5   A. E. Prince, 'The indenture system under Edward III', pp. 283-297 in Edwards; 'The payment of army wages in Edward III's reign', *Speculum* xix (1944), 137-160, H. G. Hewitt, *The Organisation of War under Edward III, 1338-62* (Manchester 1966), 33-40; see below nn. 34-6.

6   H. M. Cam, *Liberties and Communities in Medieval England* (Cambridge 1944) 214 (quoted), 205-222; see also K. B. McFarlane, ' "Bastard feudalism" ', *BIHR* xx (1943-5), 161-180.

7   K. B. McFarlane, *The Nobility of Later Medieval England* (1953, Oxford 1973), 106 (quoted), 102-121; see also J. A. Tuck, 'Richard II's system of patronage', pp. 1-20 in *The Reign of Richard II*, ed. F. R. H. Du Boulay & C. M. Barron (London 1971), pp. 15-18; R. L. Storey, 'Liveries and Commissions of the Peace', pp. 131-152 in Du Boulay, pp. 131-6.

8   P. H. Winfield, *The History of Conspiracy and Abuse of Legal Procedure* (Cambridge 1921), 150, 154 (quoted), 131-160; Holdsworth ii, 457-9, 414-6; J. Bellamy, *Crime and Public Order in England in the Later Middle Ages* (London 1973), 1-36, 199-200; A. Harding, *The Law Courts of Medieval England* (London 1973), 92-8. For complaints, see below and Ch. III, 41-45 for legislation, see *Stat. Realm* I Edw. III st. 2 c. 14, 4 Edw. III c. 11, 20 Edw. III, 1 Rich. II cc. 4, 7, 9, 7 Rich. II c. 15, 13 Rich. II st. 3, 16 Rich. II c. 4, 20 Rich. II c. 2, 1 Hen. IV c. 7.

9   W. O. Ault, 'Manors and Temporalities', iii, 3-34 in *The English Government at Work 1327-1336*, ed. W. A. Morris et al. (Medieval Academy of America 1940-1950); McFarlane, *Nobility*, 84-7, 119-121; A. L. Brown, 'The authorisation of letters under the Great Seal', *BIHR* xxxvii (1964), 125-155 (especially pp. 148-154); B. P. Wolffe, *The Royal Demesne in English History* (London 1971), 34-8, 40-51, 59-65, 72-5; Tuck, 'Patronage', 1-20.

10 McFarlane, *Nobility*, 111; see also Cam, *Liberties*, 213; see below Ch. III, 46-7, 49.

11 *Rot. Parl.* ii, 333a-b (1376), see also ii, 141a (1343), 265b (1355), iii, 44a (1377), see Winfield, 104; Storey, 131-152.

12 For duties of sheriffs, bailiffs etc., see W. Morris, 'The Sheriff', ii, 41-108, and H. M. Cam, 'Shire officials: Coroners, Constables and Bailiffs', iii, 143-183, both in Morris; Hastings, *The Court of Common Pleas in Fifteenth Century England* (Cornell 1947), 224-230. See also *Rot. Parl.* ii, 265b-266b (1355), 306a (1371), 335b (1376) etc.; *Stat. Realm* 23 Henry VI c. 9.

13 N. D. Hurnard, *The King's Pardon for Homicide before 1307* (Oxford 1969), 352-356.
14 R. B. Pugh, *Imprisonment in Medieval England* (Cambridge 1968), 224-225, 232-254; *Select Cases before the King's Council 1243-1482*, ed. I. S. Leadam & J. F. Baldwin (Seld. Soc. 35, 1918), lxxxiii-lxxxix, 54-60; *Rot. Parl.* ii, 62b-63a (1378).
15 C.II.59, 63, 179; III, 170; IV, 162.
16 Winfield, 99-102, 161-199; Holdsworth, i (4th ed. London 1927), 312-334; Hastings, 217-224; T. F. Tout, *Chapters in the Administrative History of Medieval England* (Manchester 1920-33), iii, 370-1; see *Rot. Parl.* ii, 400a (a.inc.), iii, 140b (1382); *Stat. Realm* 5 Edw.III c.10, 20 Edw.III cc.1, 6 (where 'assissours' is tr. 'Embraceors'), 34 Edw.III c.8, 38 Edw.III st.1 c.12.
17 *Rot. Parl.* ii, 287a-288b (1399)
18 *Rot. Parl.* ii, 310b made into *Stat. Realm* 46 Edw.III. See Tout iii, 282.
19 Winfield, 104, 150-1; Hastings, 231-2; Bellamy, *Crime*, 14-15; Harding, 113-114; and see *Rot. Parl.* ii, 136b-137a (1343), 259b (1354), 266a (1355), iii, 158a (1383), 200a (1384); *Stat. Realm* 20 Edw.III c.1, 8 Rich.II c.3.
20 Holdsworth, iii (5th ed. 1942), 624-5; Hastings, 211-7; *Rot. Parl.* iii, 101b-102a (1381).
21 R. H. Bowers, 'A Middle English poem on lovedays', *MLR* xlv (1952), 374-5; see also J. W. Bennett, 'The medieval loveday', *Speculum* xxxiii (1958), 351-370.
22 *Calendar of Letter Books in the City of London*, ed. R. R. Sharpe (London 1899-1912), *Letter Book D*, 283, 35-96, *Letter Book H*, 257-260; *Calendar of Plea and Memorial Rolls 1364-1381*, ed. A. H. Thomas (London 1929), liv-lvi; J. M. Imray, 'Les Bones Gentes de la Mercerye de Londres', pp.155-178 in *Studies in London History presented to P. E. Jones*, ed. A. E. J. Hollaender & W. Kellaway (London 1969), 162.
23 *Letter Book H*, 109-110.
24 Yunck, 290-1; see also Mitchell, 6; Jenkins, 128.
25 Bracton, ii, 257; *Stat. Realm* 20 Hen.III c.6; see J. M. W. Bean, *The Decline of English Feudalism 1215-1540* (Manchester 1968), 14.
26 McFarlane, *Nobility*, 11, quoting William Worcester; for *maritagia*, see Bracton, ii, 76-7, and for feoffments, *ibid*. iii, 111: '*Sciant praesentes et futuri quod ego talis dedi, concessi, et hac praesenti carta mea confirmavi tali; pro homagio et servitio suo, tantam terram cum pertinentiis in tali villa*, etcetera ut infra.' See further, Bean, 85-6; A. W. B. Simpson, *An Introduction to the History of the Land Law* (Oxford 1961), 112-4; see also C.X.250-285.
27 Bellamy, *Crime*, 58-9; see *Stat. Realm* 13 Edw.I c.35.
28 *Stat. Realm* i, 226; cp. *The Treatise on the Laws and Customs of England commonly called Glanvill*, ed. G. D. G. Hall (London 1965), 85 (vii. 12).
29 See above n.9 for royal patronage, and for wardship and marriage see Simpson, 16-19; Bean, 9-16.
30 M. McKisack, *The Fourteenth Century* (Oxford History of England v, Oxford 1959), 384-397; Tuck, *Richard II*, 20-32; Tout, iii, 287-309; see *Pol. Poems* i, 184-186, 457; *Rot. Parl.* ii, 323b-329b (1376). Meed's relation to Alice Perrers is discussed B. Huppé, 'The A-text of *Piers Plowman* and the Norman Wars', *PMLA* liv (1939), 37-64; J. A. W. Bennett, 'The date of the A-text of *Piers Plowman*', *PMLA* lviii (1943), 566-572.
31 Tout, iii, 347-384; Tuck, *Richard II*, 33-57; G. Mathew, *The Court of Richard II* (London 1968), 14-18; see complaints in *Rot. Parl.* iii, 16a (1377), 73b-74b (1379-80), 100b-101b, 115a (1381), 139a (1382).

32 *Rot. Parl.* iii, 62a (1379), 81b (1379-80), 94b (1380), 162b-163a, 212a (1385), 222b-223a (1386); cp. Ch.III n. 34 below.

33 McKisack, 444 (quoting Knighton, *Chronicon*, ii, 218-220), see also 434-447; Tout, iii, 398-418; Tuck, *Richard II*, 58-60, 87-107. See alternative dating, Jusserand, *Piers Plowman*, 56-7.

34 See n. 5 above.

35 M. M. Postan, 'The costs of the Hundred Years' War', *P & P*, xxvii (1964), 34-53 (quote p. 46), 'Some social consequences of the Hundred Years' War', *Econ. Hist. Rev.* xii (1942), 1-12; McFarlane, *Nobility*, 19-40; Hewitt, 104-110; D. Hay, 'The division of the spoils of war in fourteenth-century England', *TRHS* 5th ser., iv (1954), 91-109; M. Powicke, 'The English Aristocracy and the war', pp. 122-134 in *The Hundred Years' War*, ed. K. Fowler (London 1971), 130-132.

36 Hewitt, 106 (quoting Froissart, *Chronicles*, ed. G. C. Macaulay, London 1924, p. 95); Powicke, 130.

37 Hewitt, 99-104, 110-118; C. T. Allmand, 'The war and the non-combatant', pp. 163-183 in Fowler.

38 H. Bonet, *The Tree of Battles*, tr. and ed. G. W. Coopland (Liverpool 1949), 128-9; M. H. Keen, *The Laws of War in the Late Middle Ages* (London 1965), 63-81, 104; J. Palmer, 'The war aims of the portagonists and the negotiations for peace', pp. 5-74 in Fowler, 51-62.

39 A. Corville, 'France: the Hundred Years' War', pp. 340-367 in *The Cambridge Medieval History*, ed. J. C. Tanner et al. (Cambridge 1932), 437; but see Bennett, *Piers Plowman*, n. to B.III 188 ff, 194-5, 206.

40 Hewitt, 175-8; Allmand, 175-6; Tucker, 68-9; P. S. Lewis, 'War propaganda and historiography in Fifteenth-century France and England', *TRHS* 5th ser., xv (1965), 1-21; see e.g. *Pol. Poems* i, 58-91.

41 Bracton, ii, 335, see also 233-7; *Stat. Realm* 25 Edw.III st. 5 c. 2 (1352); see M. Bloch, *Feudal Society*, tr. M. A. Manyon (1940, 2nd edn., London 1962), 219-230; F. Pollock & F. W. Maitland, *The History of English Law before the time of Edward I* (1895, 2nd edn., Cambridge 1968), i, 298-307, 351-5; J. G. Bellamy, *The Law of Treason in England in the later Middle Ages* (Cambridge 1970), xii, 21-2, 80-85. See also C.X. 232-242 where Langland seems to be using the related doctrine of the 'corruption of blood', see Simpson, 19. See below, Ch.IV, 71-2.

Chapter III   The triumph of authority

1 *Rot. Parl.* 100b; see above Ch.II n. 8.

2 E. C. Stones, 'The Folvilles of Ashby-Folville Leicestershire, and their associates in crime, 1326-1347', *TRHS* 5th ser., vii (1957), 117-136; Bellamy, *Crime*, 69-88.

3 *Select Cases in Chancery 1364-1471*, ed. W. P. Baildon (Seld. Soc. 10, 1896), 5-6; see also *Rot. Parl.* ii, 62a (1331), 207b (1347-8).

4 See above Ch.I, 21.

5 *Fleta*, ed. H. G. Richardson & G. O. Sayles (Seld. Soc. 72, 1953/5), 109 (lib. ii c.2), tr. F. W. Maitland, 'Introduction to *Memoranda de Parliamento*', pp. 91-135 in *Historical Studies of the English Parliament*, ed. E. B. Fryde & E. Miller (Cambridge 1970), 128.

6 *Cal. Close Rolls Edw.III*, xii, 237 (1366). See Maitland, *'Mem. de Parliamento'*, 107-123; J. F. Baldwin, *The King's Council in England during the Middle Ages* (Oxford 1913); J. E. A. Joliffe, *Constitutional History of Medieval England* (London 1937), 336-341, 364-381.

7 M. Hale, *The Jurisdiction of the Lords' House* (London, ed. of 1796), 62-5, 96-112; F. Palgrave, *As Essay on the Original Authority of the King's Council* (Record Commission 1834), 19-42; *Cases in Chancery*, xvi-xxiv; Maitland, *'Mem. de Parliamento'*, 279-297; Baldwin, 236-280; *Cases before Council*, xv-xxxv; M. E. Avery, 'The history of the equitable jurisdiction of the Chancery before 1400', *BIHR* xlii (1969), 129-144; Bellamy, 100-102. A similar interpretation is advanced by T. A. Knott & D. C. Fowler in *'Piers the Plowman': a Critical Edition of the A-version* (Baltimore 1952), n. to A.III.88.

8 Ch.I n.42 above, and see Kerly, 1-36; *Cases in Chancery*, xxix-xxx, Winfield, 110; B. Wilkinson, *The Chancery under Edward III* (Manchester 1929), 47-53. *N.B.* Avery follows a distinction I am not making between 'equitable' cases (where no remedy was available at Common Law) and 'Common Law' cases (where the normal remedy could not be obtained because of poverty, maintenance etc.) — these latter constituting three quarters of the business in the fourteenth century. For a different application of 'equity' to the poem, see W. J. Birnes, *Patterns of Legality in 'Piers Plowman'* (New York University Ph.D. thesis 1974).

9 *Rot. Parl.* iii, 109b-111a (1381); see also ii, 440b (1327: against law and against all reason), 179b (1347: 'Ley & reson'), 207b-208a (1347: 'lei & reson').

10 *Cases in Chancery*, 121 ('reson et Conscience'), see also 9 ('loy et reson'), 31 ('droit et reson'), 69 ('reson et bon foy'), 119 ('ley et conscience'), 132 ('Faith, reason and conscience') etc.

11 'Of servants and lords', pp. 226-243 in *The English Works of Wyclif*, ed. F. D. Matthew (EETS os. 74, 1880, 2nd. ed. 1902), 233-5.

12 Bennett, *Manor*, 190-1 (quoting *Lives of Berkeleys*, I, 286); Hewitt, 168-172. See also *Rot. Parl.* ii, 328b-329a (1376); T. F. Plucknett, 'Parliament', pp. 82-128 in Morris, *English Government*, 117-9.

13 *Stat. Realm* 36 Edw.III st.1 c.2, but for continued complaint, see *Rot. Parl.* ii, 312a (1372), 319a-b (1373), 342b (1376), iii, 100b (1381), 115a (1381), 146b (1382) etc.

14 Pollock & Maitland, ii, 462-8; Holdsworth, ii, 256-8, 364-5, 358, 451-3; Pugh, 35-41.

15 *Rot. Parl.* iii, 42b-43a, see also 139b (1382). For similar petitions, see *Rot. Parl.* iii, 44a (1378), 62b-63a (1379), 139b-140a (1382), 662b (1411); and see Bellamy, *Crime*, 7; Winfield, 155; Jusserand, *Piers Plowman*, 34-5 treats Wrong as a Commons' spokesman for 1362 (*Rot. Parl.* ii, 269-271).

16 See n.9 above, and *Rot. Parl.* ii, 62a (1331), 267b (1355), 330a (1376), 374b-375a (1376-7), iii, 287a-288b (1391). Most of these were sent on to the Chancellor, although in the 1355 case the king said aloud, 'Jeo prenk la querele en ma main'.

17 *Cases before Council*, xi-xiv; Avery, 130. Besides cases mentioned below, see *Cases before Council*, 41-2, 81-2, 86-92, etc.; Baldwin, 520-2; the first 46 cases (pre 1400) in *Cases in Chancery* almost all involve violence and maintenance.

18 *Cases in Chancery*, 48.

19 *ibid.* p. 66-7 (*s.d.*), 83-4 (*s.d.*).

20 *Cases in Chancery*, xxxv-xlvi; Baldwin, 280-306; *Cases before Council*, xv-xlvi; Harding, 105-8, 121.

21 See above n.15 and *Stat. Realm* 2 Rich.II st.1 c.6 (Statute of Gloucester); and see Baldwin, 266-8; Winfield, 155; Pugh, 200-2. See also *Rot. Parl.* ii, 136b-137b (1343), 237a-238b (1351-2), 374b-375a (1376-7).

22 *Cal. Pat. Rolls* Rich.II, vi, 427 (1398: see *Cases before Council,* xxi); for other examples of intimidation in court, see *Select Cases in the Court of King's Bench under Edward III,* vi, ed. G. O. Sayles (Seld. Soc. 82, 1965), 64-5; *Year Bk.* 13 Hen.IV f.16.

23 Pugh, 201; *Rot. Parl.* iii, 65a (1379); *Stat. Realm* 2 Rich.II st.1 c.6.

24 *Cal. Pat. Rolls* Rich.II, vi, 597 (1399).

25 *Cases before Council,* ci-iii, 77-81; see above Ch.II, 27 (and n.10) and below Ch.III, 49 for more about Edward Courtenay.

26 The names 'Wysdom' and 'Wyt' are sufficiently similar to those of the lawyers mentioned C.IV.27 as to suggest they are also lawyers.

27 *Registrum Omnium Brevium* (London 1531), 271r-v (mainprise); Baldwin, 295; Palgrave, 44-5; *Cal. Close Rolls Rich.II* i, 486-7; G. Jacob, *A New Law Dictionary* (London 1729): BOTE, MAINPRISE.

28 *Cases before Council,* 47-8; see also *Cal. Close Rolls Edw.III* xiii, 58-9 (1369), *Rich.II* i, 486-7 (1380); *Rot. Parl.* iii, 287a-288b (1391); Palgrave, 64-5.

29 *Cases before Council,* 81 (see n.25 above); see also xlv-xlvi, lxxxiii-ix, civ-vi; Winfield, 165-6.

30 Plucknett, 'Impeachment', 64-71 (e.g. the 'Lady Meed' of 1376, Alice Perrers); *Rot. Parl.* iii, 419b (1399), see also 21a-b (1377), 44a (1378), 267b (1389); Tuck, *Richard II,* 198-200.

31 *De Offic. Reg.,* 57; see above Ch.I n.12.

32 Alford, 'Some unidentified quotations', 397-8.

33 *Rot. Parl.* iii, 446b (1399), see also 44a (1378: the Council will act when 'le Còe Loy ne purra avoir duement son cours'); Palgrave, 42-52; Baldwin, 278-280.

34 Jacob: SUPERSEDEAS; *Reg. Brev.* ff. 5, 143v-146r, 183v etc.; *Cal. Close Rolls Edw.III* xiii (1369-44), xiv (1374-7), *Rich.II* i (1377-81, e.g. pp.110-113), *passim.*

35 *Rot. Parl.* iii, 23b (1371, cp. ii, 308a), see also 221a (1387), 210a (1386); see Tout, v, 56-7, 195-211; Baldwin, 255-261; Tuck, *Richard II,* 65-70.

36 Baldwin, 320 (quoting Walsingham, *Historia Anglicana,* ii, 48); see also Birdsall, 37-55.

37 A. Steele, 'English Government Finance, 1377-1413', *EHR* li (1936), 29-51, 577-597; *Rot. Parl.* ii, 332a (1376), see also 332b, 335b, 338b, 339a, 350b (all 1376).

38 *Rot. Parl.* iii, 55a-56b (1379); see Tout, iii, 347.

Chapter IV   The Subject-kings

1 See Ch.I n.28 above.

2 On view that 'Christ the King is the theme of the last three passus', see Bloomfield, 123-9.

3 Discussed Mitchell, 12-15.

4 Holdsworth, ii, 460; see also Bennett, *Manor,* 277-317; McKisack, 312-348; Yunck, 232-7; R. H. Hilton, *The Decline of Serfdom in Medieval England* (London 1969), 32-43. For feudal contract, see Ch.II n.41 above.

5 *Stat. Realm* 23 Edw.III, 25 Edw.III st.2, 31 Edw.III st.1 c.6-7, 34 Edw.III c.9-11, 2 Rich.II st.1 c.8, 12 Rich.II c.3-10; see Holdsworth, ii, 460-4; B. Putman, *The Enforcement of the Statutes of Labourers during the First Decade after the Black Death, 1349-59* (Columbia 1908), 71-97; J. J. Jusserand, *English Warfaring Life in the Middle Ages (XIVth Century)*, tr. L. T. Smith (1889, 3rd, ed., London 1925), 263-275.

6 *Stat. Realm* 25 Edw.III st.2 c.1.

7 W. O. Ault, 'Some early Village By-laws', *EHR* xlv (1930), 208-231, esp. 213-4. Reason offers Will typical harvest work and positions (see Bennett, *Manor*, 83-4, 179-180; W. O. Ault, *Open-field Farming in Medieval England* (London 1970), 27-38, 60-3.

8 *Stat. Realm* 12 Rich.II c.3.

9 *Stat. Realm* 23 Edw.III c.1. Exception was made by 12 Rich.II c.7 for genuine men of religion; cp. C.V.90-1.

10 *Rot. Parl.* ii, 340a-341a (quote 340b), tr. R. B. Dobson, *The Peasants' Revolt of 1381* (London 1970), 72-4.

11 *Stat. Realm* 25 Edw.III st.2 c.3, 34 Edw.III c.9, 42 Edw.III c.6; see Putman, 24-6, 82-4, 181; Pugh, 38-9.

12 Jusserand, *Piers Plowman*, 112.

13 *Stat. Realm* 25 Edw.III c.2, 7, 34 Edw.III c.10, 12 Rich.II c.3, 8.

14 Putman, 91 (contravening *Stat. Realm* 25 Edw.III st.2 c.1); on effectiveness of laws see *ibid.*, 220-1. It may also have the laws' unpopularity (see McKisack, 335-6) which prompted Langland to rely more on Hunger.

15 Bennett, *Manor*, 44-6, 80; Ault, *Farming*, 22; Hilton, *Peasantry*, 20-36.

16 Postan, 'Consequences of war', 10; for the traditional model, see Mohl, 12-19, 316-323.

17 F. G. Davenport, *The Economic Development of a Norfolk Manor, 1086-1565* (London 1906), 49-55, 70-75; see also F. W. Maitland, 'The history of a Cambridgeshire manor', *EHR* ix (1894), 417-439.

18 *pace* N. Coghill, 'Langland, the "Naket", the "Nauȝty" and the Dole', *RES* viii (1932), 303-9; M. Day, '*Piers Plowman* and poor relief', *ibid.*, 445-6 (see *Stat. Realm* 23 Edw.III c.7).

19 e.g. Hebrews 10:12; Romans 3:24.

20 *Reg. Brev.*, ff. 268-274; see E. de Haas, *Antiquities of Bail* (Columbia 1940), 68-9, 85-7; cp. Ch.III n.27 above. The terms 'wed' and 'borh' are particularly associated with surety for a debt (Holdsworth, ii, 83-84), but Pollock & Maitland, ii, 169-170, 184-185 explain the looseness of such terms.

21 Tout, v, 122-133 (quote p.125); see also H. C. Maxwell-Lyte, *Historical Notes on the use of the Great Seal of England* (HMSO 1926), 1 (quoting M. Paris, *Chronica Majora* v, 130 'clavis regni'), 30-2, 313. See *ibid.* 229-234 for 'interlining', mentioned by Langland C.XIII.116-8.

22 M. C. Spalding, *The Middle English Charters of Christ* (Bryn Mawr 1914), 32; see also Wyclif, *Engl. Works*, 348. On feoffments, see Ch.II n.26 above.

23 *The Sarum Missal*, ed. J. W. Legg (Oxford 1916), 468; see R. St Jacques, 'Langland's Christ-knight and the liturgy', *Rev. Univ. Ottowa* xxxvii (1967), 146-158; (N. Bozon) *An Allegorical Romance on the Death of Christ*, ii, 427-447 in *The Chronicle of Pierre de Langtoft*, ed. T. Wright (R.S. 47, 1868), (quote p.433); W. Gaffney, 'The allegory of the Christ-Knight in *Piers Plowman*', *PMLA* xlvi (1931), 155-168.

24 Keen, *Laws*, 182; Post, 305; see also Pearsall, *Piers Plowman*, n. to C.XX.165a.

25 *The Gospel of Nicodemus, or Acts of Pilate*, Pt.II, pp.117-146 in *The Apochryphal New Testament*, ed. M. R. James (Oxford 1924); H. Traver, *The Four Daughters of God* (Bryn Mawr Monographs 6, 1907); K. Sajavaara, *The*

Middle English Translations of Robert Grosseteste's 'Chateau d'Amour' (Mémoires de la Société Néophilologique de Helsinki, 23, 1967), 62-90.

26 Pollock & Maitland, ii, 600, for a contemporary definition, see G. de Legnano, *Tractatus de Bello, de Represaliis, et de Duello* (1360), ed. T. E. Holland (Oxford 1917), 331-3, adapted in *Tree of Battles*, 198-9. On jousts, see F. H. Cripps-Day, *The History of the Tournament* (London 1918), 13-48.

27 G. Neilson, *Trial by Combat* (Glasgow 1890), 31-6, 58-62. For the third kind of duel (on appeal of felony, not discussed here), see Bracton, ii, 385-6.

28 Glanvill, 22-6 (II, 1-3); W. Blackstone, *Commentaries on the Laws of England* (1765, 3rd. ed., Dublin 1770), iii, 337-341 (XX, 5); Neilson, 46-58, 147-154; Simpson, 34-8.

29 Holdsworth, iii, 93 (quoting Pollock & Wright, *Possession*, 94-5); but see Alford, 'Literature and law', 944-5.

30 S. F. C. Milsom, *Historical Foundations of the Common Law* (London 1969), 106-114.

31 W. Dugdale, *Origines Juridicales* (London 1660), 65-71; *The Mirror of Justices*, ed. W. J. Whittaker (Seld. Soc. 7, 1895), 109-112; *Novae Narrationes*, ed. E. Shanks & S. F. C. Milsom (Seld. Soc. 80, 1963), 2-3, 25-31, 144-151. The principal's arms were painted on the champion's red silk surcoat, cp. C.XXI.12-14.

32 *Ordinances of War made by King Richard II at Durham, Ao 1385*, i, 453-8 in *The Black Book of the Admiralty*, ed. T. Twiss (R.S. 55, 1871), 453 (ii).

33 *Mirror of Justices*, 112; Glanvill, 25 (II, 3); Blackstone, iii, 340-1.

34 C. Roth, *A History of the Jews in England* (Oxford 1941), 70-3 (landlessness), 96-102 (servility and tallage); see further H. G. Richardson, *The English Jewry under Angevin Kings* (London 1960), 83-108, 161-175; see also C.XXI.34-41.

35 J. Selden, *The Dvello or Single Combat* (London 1610); Blackstone, iv, 340-2; Cripps-Day, 65-82; Neilson, 160-193; G. D. Squibb, *The High Court of Chivalry* (Oxford 1959), 1-25.

36 Neilson, 168-171, citing Walsingham, *Historia Anglicana*, i, 275, 279; *Chronicon Galfridi le Baker*, 208-210, 220-222 etc.

37 R. Barber, *The Knight and Chivalry* (London 1970), 305-313; Kantorowicz, 35 n.19; M. Keen, 'Treason trials under the Law of Arms', *TRHS* 5th ser., xii (1962), 85-104. On escheat, see above Ch.II n.41.

38 *The Ordenaunces and Fourmes of Fightyng within Lists*, i, 300-329 in *Black Book*, p.309.

39 *Cal. Close Rolls Hen.III*, iii, 6 (1234), cited Hurnard, 43-4, 176.

40 Hurnard, 15.

41 Hurnard, 16-22, 171-213.

42 See Ch.I n.28 above. Christ's faithfulness towards his brother-men can also be read in terms of 'brotherhood-in-arms', see M. H. Keen, 'Brotherhood in Arms', *History*, xlvii (1962) 1-17, and cp. C.VII.130, 141 (B.V.500), XX.20-5, XXI.12-4.

43 See Ch.I, 6, 21, n.30 above.

44 Discussed in terms of justice in Bloomfield, 130-4.

45 Gierke, 18-19, 8, 7-21; see also Lewis, 'Organic tendencies', 858-863; Chroust, 427-436; Farr, 22-29.

46 *Stat. Realm* 25 Edw.III st.5 c.2 (quoted); see Pollock & Maitland, ii, 502-8; Bellamy, *Treason*, 87-93; and see above Ch.II n.41.

47 Keen, 'Treason trials', 96; see also Keen, *Laws*, 106-8.

48 See Ch.II n.37-8 above (*dampnum*); *Ordinances of War*, 454-5 (x); Keen, *Laws*, 111 (retreat).
49 Keen, *Laws*, 119-133.
50 *Tree of Battles*, 144 (Ch.XXXIV); Prince, 'Indenture system', 290; but see Hewitt, 93.
51 *De Offic. Reg.*, 158-9; see Farr, 148.
52 Keen, *Laws*, 124-8.

(Authors of secondary sources are only indexed when referred to by name in the main text.)

reason, *cont.* 56; character in *Visio*, 1, 6, 20-3, 24, 40, 48, *50-3*, 59, 73, 75, 79; character in *Vita*, 22
redde quod debes, 1, 56, 75, 78-9
'relacoun rect', 18-20, 53-5, 57, 58, 61-2, 75, 80
retainers, 17, *25-31*, 32, 36-8, 39-45, 46, 47, 49, 53
Richard II, 1, 3, 8, 14, 26, *34-5, 51-3*, 70, 81-2
Richard Redeless, 6, 19, 22
Right, Writ of, 68-9, 71
Robertson and Huppé, 24

Samaritan, 74
Saul (King), 38
St. German, 22
Satan, 71, *see* Lucifer
Seals, Privy, 35, 51-2; Great, 64-6; *see also* letters
Secreta Secretorum, 5
sheriffs, 26, *27-30*, 39
siege, 78-9
simony, 24; character in Langland, 25, 77; *The Simonie*, 25
Sloth, 79
Solomon (King), 38
Song of Lewes, 14
soul, *16*, 21, 40, 50, 53, 55, 56, 76, 80, 81
statutes, 26, 52, 60; *see* Law
subpoena, (44), 45-7, 49
supersedeas, 30, 51-2
surety (and security), 48-9, 64-5, 77

taxation, 8-10, 28, 35, 42, 53, 70
'theocratic' monarchy, 7-12

Theology, 32-3
Trajan, 20
treason, *37-8*, 70, 71-3, *76-7*, 78-81, 98 n.41
Tree of True Love (Charity), 64, 68
truth, treuthe, *5-6*, 8, 9-11, 19, 21, 28, 56-8, 67, 69, 72, 74, 78, 95 n.36; character in Langland, 24, 33, 56-7, 58, *62-3*
tyranny, 8-10, 12, 17-18, 20, 21, 51

Unitas, 1, 9, 75-80
Unity, Principle of, 76
Usk, T., 3
usury, 31, 53

venality satire, 24-5, 32

wage, gage, *see* surety
war, 10, 25, 27; Laws, 37, 49, 70, 72, 76-9; Hundred Years' War, 25, 27, *36-8*, 53, 60 (Bretener), 78; Wars of Roses, 25; *see also* dampnum, indenture system, siege
wasters (Wastor), 1, 12, 54, 58-63, 80
Will, 22, 32, 53, 59, 65, 67
Winfield, P. H., 26
Wrong, 24, 25, 40, *42-50*, 53-4, 61, 63, 64-5, 73, 81-2
Wycliffe, J. and Wycliffites, 10, 11, 18, 42, 76; *De Offic. Reg.*, 6, 10, 51, 79, 93 n.13
Wynnere and Wastoure, 25

Yunck, J. A., 24, 32

107